MacArthur's Millennial Manifesto

A Friendly Response

Samuel E. Waldron

RBAP
Owensboro, KY

Scripture taken from the NEW AMERICAN STANDARD BIBLE®, Copyright®
1960, 1962, 1963, 1968, 1971, 1972, 1973, 1975, 1977, 1995 by The Lockman
Foundation.
Used by permission.

Requests for information should be sent to:

RBAP
1694 Wrights Landing Road
Owensboro, KY 42303
rb@rbap.net
Copies of this book may be purchased at our website www.rbap.net.
Cover design by Jeremy Bennett of www.kalosgrafx.com

Printed in the United States of America.

ISBN-13: 978-0-9802179-2-6
ISBN-10: 0-9802179-2-X

Without the vision and zeal for God's truth of two men,
this book would not have been possible:
Ted Christman and Richard Barcellos.
May God prosper every plan they have for His glory!
- Sam Waldron -

We are all in debt to Dr. Waldron for this careful and thorough refutation of John MacArthur's quixotic attempt to wed Calvinism with a form of dispensational premillennialism. With charity, this book exposes the fallacies–historical, exegetical and theological–inherent in Dr. MacArthur's presentation. While chiliasm in itself is not antithetical to some historical predestinarian theological systems, Dr. Waldron demonstrates that Calvinism does not *per se* support the argument for premillennialism as MacArthur claims. Thank you, Dr. Waldron, for showing us how a theological refutation may be done with grace and kindness.

James M. Renihan, Ph.D., Trinity Evangelical Divinity School
Professor of Historical Theology, Institute of Reformed Baptist Studies, Escondido, CA
Editor of *True Confessions: Baptist Documents in the Reformed Family*

****

Samuel Waldron's "friendly response" to John MacArthur's "millennial manifesto" will go a long way toward setting the record straight about what Reformed amillennialists actually believe about the church and Israel. It is too bad that Dr. Waldron had to write such a book, but under the circumstances, it is hard to imagine anyone doing a better job. This book is irenic. It is clear. It is judicious. Most importantly, Waldron makes a strong case that this view is the one found in Scripture. I highly recommend this book to all who are interested in this controversy.

Kim Riddlebarger, Ph.D., Fuller Theological Seminary
Senior pastor, Christ Reformed Church (URCNA), Anaheim, CA
Visiting Professor of Systematic Theology, Westminster Seminary, California
The White Horse Inn
Author of *A Case For Amillennialism*

****

Samuel Waldron's response to John MacArthur's controversial sermon, "Why Every Self-Respecting Calvinist Is a Premillennialist," is a gem. In a gentle spirit, and with an awareness of what is at stake, Waldron makes a persuasive case against MacArthur's unlikely claim that true Calvinists must subscribe to the tenets of dispensational premillennialism. Waldron is not content to make his case on the basis of history, though he does note that history is hardly on MacArthur's side—after all, the first "Calvinist,"

John Calvin of Geneva, was hardly a dispensationalist! The heart of Waldron's case lies in his careful and clear treatment of the scriptural teaching regarding Israel and the church of Jesus Christ. Rather than teaching a "supersessionist" or "replacement" theology, which regards the church as an alternative to Israel in the redemptive purpose of God, Waldron shows how the church is the new Israel, composed of Jew and Gentile alike. The church is the "Israel of God" in whom all the promises of the old covenant find their true fulfillment.

Cornelis P. Venema, Ph.D., Princeton Theological Seminary
Associate pastor, Redeemer United Reformed Church, Dyer, IN
President and Professor of Doctrinal Studies, Mid-America Reformed Seminary, Dyer, IN
Co-editor of the *Mid-America Journal of Theology*
Author of *The Promise of the Future*

****

TABLE OF CONTENTS

PART FIVE: Miscellaneous Arguments

PART SIX: Concluding Thoughts

APPENDICES

INDICES

PREFACE
John MacArthur Is My Friend!

John MacArthur is my friend. Now, I must hasten to say that he may not know it. He may not even remember me. But, I do consider him my friend. When I called my wife up for the first of a series of dates that led to our marriage, I told her it was "Sam" who was calling. Her rather deflating response was, "Sam who?" I suspect that John MacArthur might say the same thing if he was told that Sam Waldron was his friend. It is true that he has written a forward to one of my books. This very busy and useful man may remember that. I don't know. Nevertheless, lest I be mistaken for some sort of evangelical social climber, let me be clear. I consider John MacArthur my friend–but he may not know that he is.

He has been my friend ever since he took his stand against that blight on Evangelicalism known as easy-believism. He made it a burning issue and opened debate among evangelicals with his book, *The Gospel According to Jesus*. I will never cease to be grateful for this work. Easy-believism brought Evangelicalism to the brink of heresy. It demanded public rebuke and refutation. MacArthur is my friend for bringing his influence to bear on this doctrinal evil.

Furthermore, I regarded MacArthur as my friend and kindred spirit in a new way as I listened to *Grace to You* one day in my car. His sermon addressed those teachers who claim to be Christians and yet defend homosexuality and the homosexual agenda. When he closed the message in prayer, he first asked God to grant such individuals genuine repentance. Then he did something I have never heard a radio preacher do before. He launched into an imprecatory prayer in which he called down the curses of God upon such teachers. In effect, he said, "If you do not give them repentance, then bring your curses down on their heads." My heart joined with his and rejoiced in the echo of the prophetic thunder I heard in his prayer. He has been–whether he knows it or not–my deeply respected friend since that day.

I say all of this in order to make it clear that I take no delight in responding critically to MacArthur's recent manifesto in behalf of Premillennialism. He is one of my modern day heroes. I love John MacArthur and thank God for his ministry.

So, why don't I just keep my mouth shut? I suppose the short answer to that question is that there is at least one thing I love more than our dear brother. It is truth. In his opening message at the 2007 Shepherds' Conference, MacArthur set forth nothing less than a Dispensational and Premillennial manifesto. Due allowance, of course, must be made for the fact that MacArthur was preaching and not lecturing or writing. Nevertheless, his message embodies significant misrepresentations of Amillennialism and vastly confuses the true nature of the debate between Dispensational Premillennialism and Amillennialism.

Let me underscore what I have already said. Throughout this review and response to MacArthur's manifesto, I will attempt to make all due allowance for the kind of communication in which he was engaged. I do not want to misrepresent my friend or make him a sinner for a (misplaced) word in the free utterance of preaching. Note that MacArthur himself did not call what he was doing preaching. His first words were "This morning I am really not going to preach a sermon." I would not want someone to require of me the same theological precision requisite for a theological journal in the context of a sermon. Neither do I want to require this of my friend. Yet further, I do not want to misrepresent his views as badly as I think he has misrepresented mine and those of other contemporary Amillennialists.

Let me also make clear that I do not believe that my friend deliberately misrepresented us. I think he is badly misinformed. I think he has been led along a path of misconceptions by his own theological prejudices and by those who are his counselors in this matter. Truly, it is difficult for *all of us* to rightly understand and properly represent positions with which we emphatically disagree.

The fact of this tendency, however, should drive us to constant vigilance in avoiding misrepresentations. Allow me to highlight one such misrepresentation in which I believe MacArthur engaged in his message. Throughout his entire manifesto, MacArthur persistently characterized Amillennialism as holding to "replacement theology" and "supersessionism."[1] I have taken the liberty to transcribe his message and then subjected that transcription to a careful proofreading. Here is what he said according to the CD recording of his message:

> And if you say all those promises to Israel really were to the Church, they were meaningless and unintelligible to them [the Jews]. Replacement theology is what this is called, by the way, and scholastics often refer to it as supersessionism.
>
> There's no replacement theology in the theology of Jesus! There's no supersessionism.
>
> This [supersessionism] is a movement to establish that there is no earthly kingdom for Israel. That is absolutely foreign to the Old Testament and completely foreign to the New Testament.
>
> ...It's a really fine work on replacement theology. It shows the effect of this idea as forming the Church of the Dark Ages, explaining how the Church went from the New Testament concept of the Church to the sacerdotal, sacramental institutional system of the Dark Ages that we know as Roman Catholicism. Diprose lays much of that at the feet of replacement theology that rises out of Augustine and the few before him; Origin and Justin.
>
> Another effect of replacement theology is the damage that it does to Jewish evangelism.

These quotations call for a great deal of comment. Yet, for the moment, my purpose is very simple. I only want to say to MacArthur and others who think that Amillennialists embrace "replacement theology" and "supersessionism," you are wrong. The idea that the Church replaces or supersedes Israel is simply alien to the way we understand the relationship of the Old and New Israel. I will explain why in the course of this book. Here, I simply want to say I am confident that most Amillennialists today would reject "replacement theology" and "supersessionism." In fact, I only first encountered this terminology while completing my doctoral work. I

---

[1] See the first chapter which deals with the terminology–supersessionism and replacement theology.

did not know what it meant or implied, even though I had been an Amillennialist for twenty-five years. Now that I do understand the terms I can confidently say that I am an Amillennialist who rejects the whole idea that the Church replaces Israel. I also emphatically reject the kind of spiritualizing or allegorizing hermeneutic that would be necessary to defend such a view as biblical.

MacArthur and his friends are at liberty to think what they will of this. It is wrong, however, to level charges and accusations at us assuming that we hold views which we simply reject. You may think that our views logically lead to "supersessionism." They do not, but you are, I suppose, allowed to think so. But, please do not call us supersessionists when we are not and emphatically reject such views. Likewise, please do not go from bad to worse and accuse us of spiritualizing (a hermeneutic we do not hold) in order to defend a "replacement theology" which we also do not hold.

There are some whom MacArthur has angered by his manifesto. I do feel misrepresented and misunderstood by a badly misinformed brother. I am not aware, however, of being angry. In fact, this brings me to my fundamental reason for responding which is simply to set the record straight. No one who thinks he understands the Scriptures on an important point can bear to see others misrepresent views he believes are thoroughly biblical. I and my fellow Amillennialists really do believe that we have biblical eschatology right. How then can we endure seeing our views drastically misrepresented? We cannot and allegiance to the truth demands that we respond. We thank Dr. John MacArthur for making it possible, by his message, for us to set the record straight.

Sam Waldron
September 2007

CHAPTER ONE
Supersessionism and Replacement Theology

As we have noted, the terms supersessionism and replacement theology are central to the argument between MacArthur and Amillennialism. The central importance of these terms requires that they be clearly and carefully defined. Several hundred online references revealed that supersessionism and replacement theology are virtually synonymous and are used in a wide variety of contexts and discussions. Allow me to offer three observations concerning these terms.

First of all, let me clear up a matter of spelling that may be confusing to some. I found both "supercessionism" and "supersessionism" as variant spellings of the same word or concept. Since it is my belief that supersessionism is derived from the verb, supersede, I will spell it "supersessionism."[1]

Second, let me note the variety of ways and contexts in which the terminology is used. Usually (not always–I have seen it used with reference to Islam being supersessionist) the reference is related in some way to the idea that Christianity supersedes Judaism. Liberal-leaning churches today reject supersessionism as anti-Semitic. Dispensational-leaning individuals reject supersessionism as being opposed to the idea of a future restoration of Israel and asserting the replacement of Israel by the Church in the purposes of God. Conservative and especially Calvinistic Christianity (Presbyterianism in particular) is widely viewed as supersessionist. Roman Catholicism is similarly viewed as supersessionist because it replaces sacerdotal Jewish ceremonies with sacerdotal Christian ones.

---

[1] The confusion seems to stem from the fact that the Latin root *sedere* is also spelled *cedere* in Old French.

Third, let me assert that this terminology is largely pejorative in nature. At least three observations lead me to this conclusion. To begin with, my research revealed that supersessionism, as it is commonly used, conveys the theologically extreme and hermeneutically insensitive view that the Church has simply and willy-nilly replaced Israel in God's promises and purposes. Additionally, the charge of anti-Semitism associated with the accusation of supersessionism further suggests a pejorative tenor to this terminology. Finally, my own experience and study has shown that the proponents of Amillennialism or Covenant Theology do not use this terminology to describe their own position. Rather, it is clear that it is almost exclusively the opponents of our position that have developed and deployed the terminology of supersessionism and replacement theology. To be identified as a supersessionist, then, carries negative connotations similar to other labels such as "sabbatarian" and "puritanical."

For these reasons I think it best for Amillennialists to reject the terminology of supersessionism and replacement theology. Perhaps some Amillennialists have unwisely identified themselves as supersessionists. More likely, they have allowed others to characterize them in these terms without thoroughly thinking through their meaning or implications. Nevertheless, speaking for myself, I am not persuaded that this is an apt or accurate description of my theological or exegetical position. In the context of the debate between Covenant Theology and Dispensationalism, I think it extremely unwise and inaccurate for those who hold my position to describe it as supersessionism or replacement theology. Besides the pejorative tone listed above, this terminology also has linguistic connotations which I think simply misrepresent our views. A glance at a thesaurus will provide the synonyms "supplant", "replace", and "displace" for the word supersede. To say that the Church supplants, replaces, or displaces Israel does not accurately represent my view as an Amillennialist. Supersessionism and replacement theology likewise push the distortion already present in terms like "supersede" and "replace" a step further. They describe my view as erecting the unhelpful aspects of these words into a full-blown and rigorous system.

Yet, allow me to qualify my rejection of this terminology. I could, of course, speak of the Church superseding Israel with a great deal of qualification. Another of the synonyms of "supersede" according to my computer's thesaurus is "surpass." I certainly think that the Church as the New Israel surpasses the Old Israel. My point, however, is that as the butterfly surpasses the caterpillar from which it emerges, so the Church as the New Israel surpasses the Old Israel. The butterfly does not exactly replace the caterpillar. *It is the caterpillar in a new phase of existence.* In the same way, to speak of the Church replacing Israel is to forget that the Church *is* Israel in a newly reformed and expanded phase of existence. In a word, terminology like replacement theology or supersessionism disguises the biblical fact that the Church is really the *continuation* of Israel. I will argue below that there is a genetic and even physical continuity between Israel and the Church that is essential to the biblical view. I will argue that such continuity is consistent with Covenant Theology and not adequately represented by terminology like supersessionism and replacement theology.

CHAPTER TWO
All Calvinists Should Be What?

MacArthur did not claim he was preaching a sermon during the opening session of the Shepherds' Conference. His first words were, "This morning I am not going to preach a sermon." So what shall we call what MacArthur did? I have to call it something. Was it a "talk?" I don't think so. That's not what MacArthur does. It will not cause offense, I hope, if I call it a "message." It has been called many other things on the blogs and on the radio. I have heard it called "red meat for the faithful Premillennialists that will convince no one else of their position." Perhaps. I will call it simply a message or a manifesto.

The category of this event raises another interesting question. What was MacArthur trying to *do* in this message? I will discuss this in detail in my last chapter. Fundamentally, we must view this message as a manifesto (a policy, program, or proposal) in which he both attempted to call all Calvinists to become Premillennial and tell them why they should be. It is true that MacArthur states this in ways that are a little outrageous. I take this as an indication of how earnest and committed he is to his eschatology. If he is facetious at times (and I think it is much less than some others may guess) he is only half-kidding. MacArthur is dead serious about his commitment to Premillennialism. He is equally serious about commending it to Calvinistic brethren in the largest forum he can find. Personally, I think he is worried about what the future may hold for Premillennialism and what will happen to it after he is gone. He cannot in his own heart tolerate the idea of Premillenialism not dominating the Calvinistic Christianity he is helping to restore to evangelical prominence. Such is my attempt to psychoanalyze MacArthur.

The purpose of this chapter, however, is to clearly set forth the nature of his thesis and argument. His simple thesis is stated very pointedly. It is *Why Every Self-Respecting Calvinist is a Premillennialist.*

Here is the astonishing paragraph in which he states his thesis:

> Now, that leads to my title, "Why Every Self-respecting Calvinist is a Premillennialist." Now it's too late for Calvin, but it's not too late for the rest of you. [Laughter from the audience] And if Calvin were here, he would join our movement. [More laughter] But bottom line here, of all people on the planet to be Premillennialist, it should be Calvinists, those who love sovereign election. Let's leave Amillennialism for the Arminians. It's perfect. It's ideal. It's a no-brainer. God elects nobody and preserves nobody. Perfect. Arminians make great Amillennialists. It's consistent. But not for those who live and breathe the rarified air of sovereign, electing grace. That makes no sense. We can leave Amillennialism to the process theologians or the openness people who think God is becoming what He will be; and He's getting better because as every day goes by, He gets more information; and as He gets more information, He's figuring out whether or not, in fact, He can keep some of the promises He made without having to adjust all of them based upon lack of information when He originally made them. Let's leave Amillennialism to the Charismatics and the semi-Pelagians and other sorts who go in and out of salvation willy-nilly; it makes sense for their theology. Sure, Israel sinned, became apostate, killed the Son of God. That's it. Israel's out and forfeits everything. The church gets it all *if* she can do better than Israel. So far it doesn't look real hopeful.

There are many reasons to find such sentiments both astonishing and, if you are a committed Amillennialist, even outrageous. Let us, however, seek to penetrate MacArthur's rather surprising reasoning. Why does he think every Calvinist should be a Premillennialist? Or to put it in more theological terms: Why does he think Calvinism is incoherent with Amillennialism and coheres much better with Premillennialism?

MacArthur makes his reasoning clear here and in many other places in his message. He believes that Amillennialism can be reduced to the idea that the fulfillment of God's promises is wholly conditional. In other words, the fulfillment of God's promises is totally dependent on the responses of the ones to whom the promises are made. To illustrate his point, MacArthur gathers a lot of things together in a kind of conglomeration of heresy. He says that Amillennialism coheres with Arminianism, Process Theology, Open Theism and mentions Charismatics and semi-Pelagians for good measure. The point is that all of these different groups, to one extreme or another, make God's promises ultimately conditioned upon human response for their fulfillment.

But what has all this to do with Amillennialism? Here we come to the linchpin of MacArthur's reasoning. He reveals it in the closing statements of the paragraphs cited above:

> Sure, Israel sinned, became apostate, killed the Son of God. That's it. Israel's out and forfeits everything. The church gets it all *if* she can do better than Israel. So far it doesn't look real hopeful.

MacArthur regards Amillennialism as teaching that Israel has finally forfeited all God's promises by their disobedience. Consequently, they lost their original status as God's people. These promises have been transferred to the Church, which MacArthur assumes from within his Dispensational mindset is a completely different entity than Israel. This view he thinks ignores and impugns God's sovereign election by teaching that Israel could forfeit their status as the elect nation. This, says MacArthur, is nothing more or less than the essential and flawed view of election held by Arminians.

This line of reasoning underscores the importance of MacArthur's claim that Amillennialism is replacement theology and supersessionism. In the Preface, I highlighted the centrality of supersessionism in MacArthur's misrepresentation of Amillennialism. Now we can see why this element is so central. The charge of supersessionism *must* necessarily be true in order to support MacArthur's claim that Amillennialism assumes an Arminian view of election. In other words, the charge of supersessionism is the foundational assumption of his main argument. Proof may be found in many places in his manifesto. Perhaps, however, the clearest statement for our purposes here is found at the conclusion of his message. Note especially the words that I have italicized in the following quotation:

Another effect of replacement theology is the damage that it does to Jewish evangelism. Here's a little scenario: You are talking to a Jew. You say, "Jesus is the Messiah." "Really, where is the kingdom?" "Oh, it's here!" "Oh, it is? Well, why are we being killed all the time? Why are we being persecuted and why don't we have the land that was promised to us? And why isn't the Messiah reigning in Jerusalem, and why isn't peace and joy and gladness dominating the world, and why isn't the desert blooming and...?" "Oh, no, you don't understand. All that's not going to happen. *You see, the problem is you're not God's people any more. We are.*" "Oh! I see, but this is the kingdom, and Jews are being killed and hated, and Jerusalem is under siege. This is the kingdom? If this is the kingdom, Jesus is not the Messiah. He can't be. It's ludicrous." No matter how many wonderful Jewish-Christian relationships we try to have with rabbis, this is a huge bone in the throat. Why can't Jesus be the Messiah? Because this isn't the kingdom. Unless you can say to a Jew, "God will keep every single promise He made to you, and Jesus will fulfill every single promise, and that is why there are still Jews in the world, and that is why you are in the land and God is preparing for a great day of salvation in Israel; and Jesus is your Messiah. But look at Psalm 22 and Isaiah 53 and Zechariah 12:10 and understand that He had to come and die to ratify the New Covenant before He could forgive your sin, and the kingdom is coming," you don't have a chance to communicate. The rest doesn't make sense. *Now, if you get election right–divine, sovereign, gracious, unconditional, unilateral, irrevocable election–and you get God right, and you get Israel right, and you get eschatology right, then guess what, men, you can just open your Bible and preach your heart out of that text and say what it says.*

Once again, my point is simply that MacArthur views Amillennialism as cohering with Arminianism because of his claim that it teaches replacement theology.

All this brings us to a second prominent feature in MacArthur's reasoning. It is the claim that Amillennialism holds a spiritualizing or allegorizing hermeneutic. Because MacArthur assumes that modern Amillennialists hold replacement theology (i.e., are supersessionists), he charges them with a spiritualizing or allegorizing hermeneutic. In his view, Amillennialists are guilty of substantially denying that God keeps His promises. Note the following quotations:

Is in fact working hard to understand prophetic passages needless, even impossible, because they require a spiritualized or allegorized set of interpretations that says the truth is somehow hidden behind the normal meaning of the words so any idea of what it might mean is as good as any other idea of what it might mean since it doesn't mean what it says?

But the idea that the New Testament is the starting point for understanding the Old Testament is exactly where Amillennialism comes from, reading it back into the Old Testament; and, of course, you damage the perspicuity or the clarity of the sensibility of the Old Testament in and of itself. Such an approach leads to an even more grand kind of spiritualizing that goes beyond just prophetic texts and gives license to spiritualize other things and to read New Testament Christian principles back into those texts in the Old Testament where they do not rise from a legitimate interpretation.

Now, the question of hermeneutics and the substance of MacArthur's thesis will be critically examined in the chapters to come. The purpose of this chapter is to make sure we all understand what his thesis is. MacArthur's thesis really is summed up clearly in the title of his message. His title encompasses or entails the main arguments or assumptions of his message. Let me briefly review it under several bullet points:

- ❖ Every Calvinist should be a Premillennialist (main thesis).
- ❖ Because Amillennialism is essentially Arminian in its view of election.
- ❖ Because Amillennialism holds replacement theology which teaches that Israel lost God's promises through their sin and was replaced by the Church.
- ❖ Thus, Amillennialism must be guilty of the horrible hermeneutic of spiritualizing or allegorizing literal promises made to Israel into spiritual promises made to the Church.

If this reasoning is correct, then I think MacArthur's astonishing claim that *Every Calvinist should be a Premillennialist* makes a kind of logical sense. If his claims about Amillennialism are true, his conclusions follow in a fairly logical way. In the chapters to come this line of reasoning must, therefore, be carefully examined.

CHAPTER THREE
MacArthur Versus Church History

Before diving into an analysis of MacArthur's thesis, I think it is important to interject a brief consideration of historical issues. In this chapter and the next we will deal with the question of how MacArthur's manifesto squares with church history.

Specifically, I want to discuss two issues. First, I want to note the interesting way in which church history fails to corroborate MacArthur's views. Second, I want to clarify the true nature of MacArthur's views and the historical debate into which he has chosen to enter.

In this chapter my point is that church history fails to corroborate MacArthur's views. From one standpoint, I am saying nothing controversial here at all. MacArthur himself admits this fact in the introduction to his message. Listen to him again:

> I want to begin with a sentence that I am going to read to you. It's a very long sentence so don't hold your breath waiting for a period. "It is one of the strange ironies in the Church and in Reformed theology that those who love the doctrine of sovereign election most supremely and most sincerely, and who are most unwavering in their devotion to the glory of God, the honor of Christ, the work of the Spirit in regeneration and sanctification, the veracity and inerrancy of Scripture, and who are the most fastidious in hermeneutics, and who are the most careful and intentionally biblical regarding categories of doctrine, and who see themselves as guardians of biblical truth and are not content to be wrong at all, and who agree most hardily on the essential matters of Christian truth so they labor with all their powers to examine in a Berean fashion every relevant text to discern the true interpretation of all matters of divine revelation, are–that's the main verb–in varying degrees of disinterest in applying those

passions and skills to the end of the story and rather content to be
in a happy and even playful disagreement in regard to the vast
biblical data on eschatology as if the end didn't matter much."
Period.

Or, another way to say it would be how many of you have
attended an Amill prophecy conference? [Laughter from the
audience]

Notice how MacArthur emphasizes that it is strange to him that the
Covenant Theologians who most celebrated sovereign election were
generally not Premillennial. Certainly, they were not the same kind
of Premillennialist as MacArthur. Rather, Covenant Theologians
historically tended to be Amillennial.

In the same vein, we must not fail to quote one of the most
controversial remarks that MacArthur made during his message:

Now that leads to my title: "Why Every Self-Respecting Calvinist
is a Premillennialist." Now it's too late for Calvin, but it's not too
late for the rest of you. [Laughter from the audience] And if Calvin
were here, he would join our movement. [More laughter] But
bottom line here, of all people on the planet to be Premillennialist,
it should be Calvinists, those who love sovereign election.

Now, I am not upset about MacArthur's remark that Calvin would
have been a Premillennialist in our day. As outrageous as this
statement may be, I suppose he may have said it in jest. It certainly
is completely incapable of historical demonstration. My purpose,
however, is simply to note what MacArthur straightforwardly admits
here. John Calvin was not a Premillennialist. Beyond Calvin, the
majority of Calvinists historically until today have not been
Premillennialists either.

Of course, much more could be said along this line. MacArthur
likewise admits elsewhere that Augustine was not in favor of his
eschatology. Instead, in MacArthur's view, he was a proponent
(horrors) of replacement theology. He said, "Diprose lays much of
that at the feet of the replacement theology that rises out of
Augustine and the few before him; Origen and Justin." Augustine is
commonly understood and acknowledged to be the one who set the
Church on an Amillennial course for over a thousand years by
abandoning Premillennialism and defending an Amillennial

interpretation of Revelation 20. The key passage is found in the *City of God,* Book 20, chapters 6-10.[1]

What has MacArthur calmly admitted in these statements? He has admitted that the major historical defenders of his understanding of sovereign grace and election have consistently rejected his eschatology. MacArthur thinks that Calvinistic views of election ought to lead–in fact, must logically and clearly lead–to Premillennial views of eschatology. Yet, and in stunning contrast, Church history shows just the opposite connection. The major proponents of sovereign election have been also the major advocates of Amillennialism. Augustine almost single-handedly opposed the insidious and centuries-long drift of the early church into Pelagianism. The view of sovereign election held by MacArthur is commonly known by the very name of Calvin. Calvin's theological descendants have been its major and sometimes lonely defenders in the modern era. Furthermore, the very modern age that marked the rise of Premillennialism also marked the *fall* of Calvinism. Yet, in spite of all this, MacArthur tells us that Calvinism, in a clear and logical way, leads to Premillennialism.

Now, I must hasten to admit that Church history confronts us at times with some very strange doctrinal spectacles and some very self-contradictory theologies. Some theologies seem to be like mythological creatures that are both fish and fowl and both man and beast. I never cease to be amazed at the prevalence of Dispensationalism among Pentecostals–when their views of the miraculous gifts ought to dispose them to any eschatology but that. I recently had a conversation with a college professor of biblical studies, a Pentecostal himself, who admitted this to be a strange inconsistency. I have also observed Baptists who against all reason were Theonomists. Similarly, it is well-known that some of the early Dispensationalists like L.S. Chafer were–of all things–Presbyterians.

---

[1] One of my correspondents pointed out that the Church was dominantly Roman Catholic for this millennium and that Roman Catholicism is Amillennial. This is supposed to be an argument against Amillennialism. Not only does this forget that Luther and Calvin remained Amillennial when leaving Rome, it also forgets that this kind of argument is a two-edged sword. Yes, we have most Roman Catholics on our side, but the Premillenialist has the Jehovah's Witnesses, Seventh Day Adventists, and the Church of Jesus Christ of Latter-Day Saints as fellow Premillennialists. The point is that this kind of argumentation proves nothing. It is guilt by association.

My purpose is not to offend any who might read this and who hold together doctrines that are, in my opinion, so incoherent. My point is simply that the figures and events of Church history do not always display logical congruity.[2]

I acknowledge that Church history is not our final authority. I also admit that we must be careful what we deduce from Church history. But having acknowledged all this, it still seems to me that Church history and historical theology generally reflects a certain logical progression. There was a reason why the canon had to be settled (basically) before its doctrinal contents could be debated. There was a reason why Nicea's doctrine of Christ's deity had to precede Chalcedon's doctrine of the Person of Christ. There was a reason why Augustine's doctrine of man, sin, and grace had to precede Luther's doctrine of faith alone and Calvin's doctrine of sovereign grace. There was a reason why Chalcedon's doctrine of the Person of Christ had to precede Anselm's *Cur Deus Homo* (*Why God Became Man*) with its new clarity regarding the atonement.

Church history displays, however imperfectly, a certain logical progression in its developments. It does so because both the divine Spirit that guides it and the human spirits that populate it are rational and logical. This means that MacArthur's admissions about the actual state of Church history with regard to his thesis cannot be lightly disregarded. Augustine, Calvin, and their theological descendants have exercised centuries-long influence because their writings were both pervasively biblical and consistently logical. They never saw–on the contrary, they pointedly rejected–the idea that sovereign election leads clearly and logically to Premillennialism. If this matter is as clear as MacArthur suggests, why did such great theological minds consistently fail to grasp it?

---

[2] My mention of self-contradictory theologies provoked an interesting exchange about the description, "Reformed Baptist." Someone asked if we shouldn't include "Reformed Baptist" in a list of such theologies and asserted that historically the name is self-contradictory. Another responded by asking what is contradictory about being reformed and baptistic? He went on to argue (in my opinion cogently) that the early, historic, Baptist confessions suggest otherwise.

CHAPTER FOUR
MacArthur - Leaky Dispensationalist

The fact that Church history fails to corroborate MacArthur's view that Calvinism logically leads to Premillennialism is not the only historical observation to consider. Additionally, a clarification of the true nature of MacArthur's views and the historical debate into which he has chosen to enter is needed. This clarification, when set in the context of centuries of Christian thought, highlights even further the historical incongruity of MacArthur's position.

So what is the true nature of his view? It is generally known that MacArthur would classify himself as a kind of Dispensationalist. I think he embraces the description "leaky Dispensationalist."[1] Yet, it is interesting to note that MacArthur deliberately avoids presenting his teaching as Dispensationalism in this message. It is clear on this occasion that he wants to be viewed as a representative of main-line Premillennialism. Consider the following comments:

> Now at this point, I feel the vibe coming from those of you who are saying, "Oh no, we came to a pastors' conference, and it's turned into a Dispensational conference. Next thing he's going to do is drag out Clarence Larkin charts, and we're going to get a really nice leather-bound Scofield Bible, and then we're all going to get the *Left Behind* series. Ah, we're reduced to rapture fiction. Then he's probably going to tell us there are seven dispensations, two kingdoms, two new covenants, two ways of salvation." Relax. [Laughter from audience] Forget Dispensationalism. I'm not talking about that...

---

[1] This description of himself may be found on the internet at this link http://www.biblebb.com/files/macqa/70-16-9.htm.

I confess I reject the wacky world of newspaper exegesis. I reject the cartoon eschatology: the crazy interpretations like the locusts of Revelation 9 being helicopters and crazy things like that. If you preach that, take that out of the tape. . . But let me tell you something, folks, as wacky as that world of Dispensational eschatology can be, it is no more wacky than the interpretation of many Amillennialists…

You say, well, didn't the Dispensationalists invent Premillennialism? Well, in the modern era two books really reintroduced Premillennial views–the straightforward biblical view–and neither of them were written by a Dispensationalist. The first one was called *The Premillennial Advent*. It was written in 1815 by an Anglican named William Cunningham. The second one that reintroduced this into the more modern era was a publication in England in 1827 written by Emmanuel de Lacunza y Diaz; a Jesuit. So there is not a necessary connection between all that is strange in Dispensationalism and this clear understanding of the kingdom.

One of the wacky ideas of Dispensationalism is that Jesus came and offered a kingdom, and because the Jews didn't accept it and killed him, He went to the Church. He came up with Plan B. The Cross is not Plan B.

I suggest for your reading *Israel and the Church* by Ronald Diprose. We should have some in the bookstore. It first appeared in Italian. It was a Ph.D. dissertation. It has no connection to traditional Dispensationalism. It's a really fine work on replacement theology.

Additionally, the only positive comment I can find about Dispensationalism in the entire message is the following:

I'm not talking about that, even though every one of you is a Dispensationalist. You are! You believe that God dealt with man one way before the fall, after the fall, before the Law, after the Law, before the Cross, after the Cross, now and in eternity, right? Okay, that's what I thought. [Laughter from the audience]

These comments represent all of MacArthur's references to Dispensationalism by name. It seems quite clear that MacArthur is eager to present himself merely as a simple Premillennialist in this message. He does not wish to be viewed as defending Dispensationalism in it.

Now from a certain perspective, who can fault him for this? No doubt, he believes that much of what he calls the wacky world of Dispensationalism is nonsensical, indefensible, and quite distinct from historic Premillennialism. I agree with this assessment. In fact, I admit that Historic Premillennialism has little or nothing to do with the fables of modern Dispensationalism.

On the other hand, an important fact gets lost in MacArthur's eagerness to distance himself from Dispensationalism. For instance, MacArthur's comments may obscure the fact that he is still defending a form of Premillennialism that only Dispensationalists hold. Why do I say this? Well, as we have seen, MacArthur builds his entire argument on a rejection of replacement theology and supersessionism. In the process of his argument, he makes this interesting admission, "Diprose lays much of that at the feet of replacement theology that rises out of Augustine and the few before him; Origen and Justin." It is the little reference to Justin that is arresting. Justin is Justin Martyr. Justin Martyr is one of the premier examples of early Premillennialism. Yet, as an early Premillennialist, he held replacement theology, according to Diprose and (assumedly) MacArthur.

This assessment is true in certain sense. Justin Martyr clearly believed that the Church and not physical Israel was the true Israel and heir of the millennial kingdom. The following statement from chapter 11 of *The Dialog with Trypho the Jew* is representative of many:

> For the true spiritual Israel, and descendants of Judah, Jacob, Isaac, and Abraham...are we who have been led to God through this crucified Christ...[2]

Irenaeus, the other leading light of early Premillennialism, by common consent also held what MacArthur calls supersessionism.[3] In fact, what we know of all early, Historic Premillennialism leads

---

[2] See for many more such statements *The Dialog with Trypho the Jew*, chapters 11, 120, 123, 125, 135.
[3] See Irenaeus' *Against Heresies*, Book 5, Chapters 32-35.

to the conclusion that it consistently rejected the Church/Israel distinction of Dispensationalism.[4]

Dispensationalism's distinction between the Church and Israel only seems to have risen in the nineteenth century. Apparently, it seemed quite novel to Charles Spurgeon. Spurgeon declared:

> ...we have even heard it asserted that those who lived before the coming of Christ do not belong to the church of God! We never know what we shall hear next, and perhaps it is a mercy that these absurdities are revealed one at a time, in order that we may be able to endure their stupidity without dying of amazement.[5]

Let me hasten to say that I am not calling anybody stupid. Neither am I saying that Dispensationalism's Church/Israel distinction is stupidity. Those are Spurgeon's words, not mine. All I am doing is showing what one mid-19th century Premillennialist thought of the idea that the Church and Israel were two distinct peoples of God.[6]

What is my point? Historic Premillennialism–the Premillennialism of the Early Church period–held what MacArthur chooses to describe as supercessionism. In light of this fact, MacArthur (unintentionally I am sure) misrepresents the real state of the historical debate when he paints the issue as Premillennialism versus Amillennialism. It is not Premillennialism versus Amillennialism. It is Dispensational Premillennialism (which is what MacArthur holds) versus Historic Premillennialism (also and significantly known as Covenant Premillennialism). It is, in fact, Dispensationalism versus everybody else. Why? Because everybody else holds a version of what MacArthur calls replacement theology or supersessionism. It is Dispensational Premillennialism versus Historic Premillennialism, Amillennialism, and Postmillennialism.

---

[4] It may be good to note here that it is common for Dispensationalists to make the claim that the early church was Premillennial. I think the evidence clearly points to a different conclusion. The early church was split between Historic Premillennialism and Amillennialism. Cf. chapter 2 of my book, *The End Times Made Simple* (Amityville, NY: Calvary Press, 2003) where I give the evidence for this conclusion.

[5] Iain Murray, *The Puritan Hope* (London: The Banner of Truth Trust, 1971), 259.

[6] Though the idea that Spurgeon was Premillennial is controversial, I accept it.

Again, let's be clear about the nature of the debate. It is not mainline Premillennialism against Amillennialism and Postmillennialism (lumped in with Amillennialism by MacArthur). It is MacArthur's version of Premillennialism–a Dispensational version of Premillennialism–against every other view held by orthodox Christians throughout the centuries. It is important to have a clear understanding of this as we proceed to examine the scriptural merits of MacArthur's arguments and assumptions.

CHAPTER FIVE
Not Your Father's Amillennialism

I have my doubts about whether Reformed Amillennialists have ever really taught what MacArthur calls replacement theology or supersessionism. Of course, I do not deny that Roman Catholic Amillennialists may have been supersessionists. I also do not deny there have been Amillennialists who were anti-Semitic and for this reason were, in the worst sense, supersessionists. There also, however, have been Premillennialists—and not a few—who belonged to heretical cults. Now, this does not make Premillennialism cultic. Neither does the anti-Semitism of some Amillennialists and the supersessionism of Roman Catholicism make Amillennialism necessarily supersessionist.

But here I want to leave aside the question of whether Amillennialism ever really held replacement theology or supersessionism. Even *if* some did *once*, this charge is certainly not appropriate today. Thus, I admit that there has been development within Amillennialism, thanks in part, to its interaction and discussion with Dispensationalism. Of course, there has also been development (it should go without saying to anyone who knows the current fractured Dispensational scene) within Dispensationalism. There are Classic, Modified, and Progressive Dispensationalists and sub-divisions in each category. Each will give you a different take on what Dispensationalism means to them. Indeed, MacArthur has distanced himself from Classic Scofield Dispensationalism in many ways and at many times.

The reality of such development within both Amillennialism and Dispensationalism highlights a serious defect in MacArthur's message. The only "Amillennialists" that MacArthur quotes in his sermon are O.T. Allis, Floyd Hamilton, and Loraine Boettner. This is a defect that cannot be overlooked. Note what MacArthur sets forth as representative of Amillennialism:

> O.T. Allis, a well-known Amillennialist, writing in *Prophecy and the Church* says, "The Old Testament prophecies, if literally interpreted, cannot be regarded as having been yet fulfilled or being capable of fulfillment in the present age." That was a problem for him.

> Floyd Hamilton in *The Basis of the Millennial Faith* said, "Now we must frankly admit that a literal interpretation of the Old Testament prophecies gives us just such a picture of an earthly reign of the Messiah as the Premillennialist pictures."

> Another Amillennialist, Loraine Boettner in *The Meaning of the Millennium*, said, "It is generally agreed that if the prophecies are taken literally, that they do foretell a restoration of the nation of Israel in the land of Palestine with the Jews having a prominent place in that kingdom and ruling over the other nations."

The works of these three authors were written in 1945, 1942, and 1958, respectively. I think it is legitimate to respond to the citation of such dated materials by asking this question. How would MacArthur like it if I cited the (old) Scofield Reference Bible or the Classic Dispensational authors and assumed that he held their position? He would think (and rightly so) that this is quite unfair. Similarly, we think the same thing when, after all the development in the defense and articulation of Amillennialism over the last fifty years, books that are sixty-two, sixty-five, and forty-nine years old (as of 2007) are quoted as representative of our position.

Additionally, it is important to my case to notice how especially incredible it is that MacArthur cites Boettner as a supersessionist Amillennialist. Why? Because Boettner was a Postmillennialist. I'll explain below what makes that so important. However, lest I be misunderstood, let me say that I am sure that MacArthur knows Boettner is a Postmillennialist. I am not charging him with ignorance on this point. The simple fact is that MacArthur deliberately and knowingly lumps Postmillennialists in with Amillennialists. Early in his message he made his viewpoint clear:

There are a number of Amillennialists who feel that way; and, by the way, we will talk just in broad terms about Amillennialism. (If any Postmillennialists are left out, you can simply attach to yourself the new label for Postmillennialism which is "optimistic Amillennialism" because the two positions are basically the same. Whether you are a Postmillennialist or an Amillennialist, you are saying that the kingdom, as identified in the Old Testament and promised to Israel, will not happen. You are either saying that the kingdom will never be literally on earth [Amill] or that it will be replaced by another kind of kingdom which will take place on earth [Postmill]. In either case, you are denying the literal fulfillment of the promised kingdom to Israel.)

I am clear, then, on the fact that MacArthur knows Boettner is a Postmillennialist. Yet, he thinks it does not make any difference for his purposes. MacArthur is mistaken. Here's why. Remember the major thesis that MacArthur is asserting? He repeatedly states that Amillennialists do not believe God really keeps His promises to Israel. He deduces this from the supposed fact that they are supersessionists who believe that the Church displaced Israel in God's promises. Here is the problem. Everybody knows that Postmillennialists almost universally hold to the future, national conversion of ethnic Israel in conjunction with their understanding of the millennium.[1] MacArthur ought to have known this. He probably does know this.

Surely, then, the charge of supersessionism begins to appear very hollow when it is made against an eschatological view which generally holds to a future mass conversion of Israel. MacArthur also holds the same hope. So, how is someone who holds a future national conversion of ethnic Israel, on the basis of the promises of the Bible, guilty of teaching that God will not keep His promises to ethnic Israel? What kind of justice is there in charging such an eschatological viewpoint with replacement theology or superessionism?

Doubtless, some may be ready to respond by pointing out that Amillennialists do not hold to such a future conversion of Israel. They may think that the charge of supersessionism or replacement theology at least applies to Amillennialists (including me). The

---

[1] Iain Murray, *The Puritan Hope* (London: The Banner of Truth Trust, 1971), 41ff.

following questions/accusations may be leaping to the lips of some readers. "Do you not deny that Romans 11, for instance, teaches a future national conversion of Israel?" "Do you not teach that "all Israel" in Romans 11 is simply all the elect?" "Is this not clear evidence of supersessionism?"

Let me answer these questions straightforwardly. *"Do you not deny that Romans 11, for instance, teaches a future national conversion of Israel?"* True enough, I do not think that Romans 11 teaches a future *national* conversion of Israel. *"Do you not teach that "all Israel" in Romans 11 is simply all the elect?"* No, I do not think that in Romans 11 "all Israel" is all the elect or spiritual rather than ethnic Israel. Surprised? You shouldn't be. The *"all Israel is all the elect"* interpretation may not even be the majority viewpoint among contemporary Amillennialists. Let me add that, even if it were, I do not think that it would be clear evidence of supersessionism. The fact of the matter is, however, that many Amillennialists today, as well as in the past, hold the view that Israel refers to ethnic Israel in Romans 11.

Some who read this may be shocked by and even disbelieve this news. I know I have some explaining to do. So let me explain. Among those that MacArthur lumps together as Amillennialists, there are at least three views of the meaning of "all Israel" in Romans 11:25-26. These views are delineated by Anthony Hoekema in *The Bible and the Future*.[2] I say this partly because, if MacArthur had correctly represented contemporary Amillennialism, he would have quoted someone like Hoekema–not Allis or Hamilton. The three views Hoekema delineates are (1) the "future national conversion of ethnic Israel" view, (2) the "all the elect from both Gentiles and Jews–who are spiritual Israel" view, and (3) the "total number of the elect from among ethnic Israel" view.

Admittedly, all three of these views have been held by Reformed Amillennialists.[3] The first view is also commonly held by Dispensationalists. Both the first and third views regard Israel in Romans 11 as referring to ethnic Israel. Consequently, the first and third views regard Romans 11 as predicting the conversion of ethnic

---

[2] Anthony A. Hoekema, *The Bible and the Future* (Grand Rapids: Eerdmans, 1979), 239-241.

[3] The first view was that of John Murray, *Romans* (Grand Rapids: Eerdmans, 1968), *ad loc*, and the mass of Postmillennialists.

Israelites and therefore cannot be guilty of supersessionism. Only with regard to the second view is there even a superficial reason to make the charge of supersessionism.[4] But, here is the striking reality. Anthony Hoekema, the Amillennialist, chooses the *third* view which says that only the elect from among ethnic Israelites is in view. Listen to what he says:

> A third interpretation of the clause in question understands it as describing the bringing to salvation throughout history of the total number of the elect from among the Jews...

> The interpretation of the words "and so all Israel will be saved" which does most justice to the Scriptural givens is the third.[5]

This is no unusual or eccentric viewpoint peculiar to Hoekema. Many contemporary Amillennialists, and some not so contemporary, also hold this exegetical position. Other subscribers, to give a short list, are O. Palmer Robertson,[6] William Hendriksen,[7] Herman Bavinck,[8] and even (a little surprisingly) the defender of postmillennialism, Loraine Boettner.[9]

What is the point? The point is that many Amillennialists believe in one way or another Romans 11 predicts the future conversion of ethnic Jews. Doesn't it seem, therefore, a little inept and inappropriate to describe such a view as holding replacement theology or as being supersessionist? Yet, MacArthur repeatedly charges Amillennialists with saying that God has set aside his promises to Israel because of their unbelief. I have italicized the most relevant statements in the following quotation:

---

[4] The second view was that of John Calvin, *Commentaries, ad loc.*

[5] Hoekema, The Bible and the Future, 240-241.

[6] O. Palmer Robertson, *The Israel of God* (Phillipsburg, NJ: P&R Publishing, 2000), 167ff.

[7] William Hendriksen, *The Bible and the Life Hereafter* (Grand Rapids: Baker, 1959), 146-149.

[8] Herman Bavinck, *The Last Things* (Grand Rapids: Baker, 1996), 106.

[9] Loraine Boettner, *The Millennium* (Philadelphia: The Presbyterian and Reformed Publishing Company, 1957), 310-321, seems to take a view of Romans 11 that favors the third view delineated by Hoekema. I must say, however, that he does not comment on Romans 11:25-26 explicitly and his view seems to combine elements of the second view with the third.

Now, that leads to my title: "Why Every Self-Respecting Calvinist is a Premillennialist." Now it's too late for Calvin, but it's not too late for the rest of you. [Laughter from audience] And if Calvin were here, he would join our movement. [More laughter] But bottom line here, of all people on the planet to be Premillennialist, it should be Calvinists, those who love sovereign election. Let's leave Amillennialism for the Arminians. It's perfect. It's ideal. It's a no-brainer. God elects nobody and preserves nobody. Perfect. Arminians make great Amillennialists. It's consistent. But not for those who live and breathe the rarified air of sovereign, electing grace. That makes no sense. We can leave Amillennialism to the process theologians or the openness people who think God is becoming what He will be; and He's getting better because as every day goes by, He gets more information; and as He gets more information, He's figuring out whether or not, in fact, He can keep some of the promises He made without having to adjust all of them based upon lack of information when He originally made them. Let's leave Amillennialism to the Charismatics and the semi-Pelagians and other sorts who go in and out of salvation willy-nilly; it makes sense for their theology. *Sure, Israel sinned, became apostate, killed the Son of God. That's it. Israel's out and forfeits everything.* The church gets it all *if* she can do better than Israel. So far it doesn't look real hopeful.

But for those of us who get it, that God is sovereign and that He is the only one who can determine who will be saved and when they will be saved, and He is the only one who can save them, *Amillennialism makes no sense because it basically says Israel, on its own, forfeited all the promises.* Do you think, on their own, they could've done something to guarantee they'd receive them? What kind of theology is that? That's Arminian theology.

This is not what Amillennialists teach at all. Rather, they teach that God is continuing to fulfill His promises to Israel in the ongoing and future conversion of (at least a remnant of) ethnic Israelites. In direct contradiction to MacArthur's claims, they do not teach that this conversion ultimately depends on Israel's faith, but on God's electing grace. The difference, therefore, between MacArthur and Amillennialism is not whether God keeps His promises to ethnic Israel. Furthermore, the difference is certainly not whether God's promises to ethnic Israel are finally conditioned on an unaided human response to them.

Excursus: Are Contemporary Amillennialists Supersessionists?

One of my correspondents pointed out a number of quotations from the book *Continuity and Discontinuity* that seem to indicate an embrace of replacement theology among contemporary Amillennialists. This correspondent pointed out that toward the end of his discussion of the relationship between Israel and the Church, Amillennialist Marten Woudstra writes:

> The question whether it is more proper to speak of a replacement of the Jews by the Christian Church or of an extension (continuation) of the OT people of God into that of the NT church is variously answered. Some prefer to think in terms of growth of the church out of OT Israel. There is biblical warrant for this. But it is also true that Jesus says that the owner of the vineyard (read 'OT Israel') will let out the vineyard to other tenants (Matthew 21:41). This shows that along with continuity there is discontinuity between OT Israel.[10]

Later in the same book, Amillennialist Bruce Waltke writes:

> As the obverse side of the NT coin bears the hard imprint that no clear passage teaches the restoration of national Israel, its reverse side is imprinted with the hard fact that national Israel and its law have been permanently replaced by the church and the New Covenant. Without wresting Matthew 15:13 and Mark 12:1-9, our Lord announced in these passages that the Jewish nation no longer has a place as the special people of God; that place has been taken by the Christian community which fulfills God's purpose for Israel.[11]

The correspondent affirmed that he often comes across the terminology of "replacement" in the writings of Amillennialists. He also cited the book, *The Israel of God in Prophecy: Principles of*

---

[10] Marten H. Woudstra, "Israel and the Church: A Case for Continuity" in *Continuity and Discontinuity: Perspectives on the Relationship Between the Old and New Testaments,* ed. John S. Feinberg (Westchester, IL: Crossway Books, 1988), 237.

[11] Bruce K. Waltke, "Kingdom Promises as Spiritual" in *Continuity and Discontinuity*, 274-275.

Prophetic Interpretation by Hans K. LaRondelle. LaRondelle writes:

> This solemn decision [in Matthew 21:43] implies that Israel would no longer be the people of God and would be replaced by a people that would accept the Messiah and His message of the kingdom of God...In short, His Church...would replace the Christ-rejecting nation. [12]

This correspondent concluded that he recognized that not all Amillennialists fall into the category of supersessionists, but many certainly do.

Another correspondent replied by saying that part of the problem with the term, supersessionism, was the failure to distinguish corporate Israel from individual Israelites. He argued that corporate Israel as the embodiment of the kingdom of God clearly was superseded by the Church. "Therefore I say to you, the kingdom of God will be taken from you and given to a nation bearing the fruits of it" (Matthew 21:43). The Church as a corporate entity became the new covenant holy nation superseding Israel (1 Peter 2:9-10). He went on to say that within that corporate entity of the Church we find both Jews and Gentiles in abundance. Thus, God is fulfilling His promise to "the remnant" and in this fashion "all Israel" is being saved. The Dispensationalist error is in requiring a future corporate restoration of Israel as the sole people of God.

A different correspondent replied to the effect that the above quotes do not establish the point that MacArthur argued against. He commented that it seems on one level there is a kind of replacement taking place and Covenant theologians recognize this, but do not embrace the kind of separation that MacArthur has in mind. He said that for MacArthur's arguments to work there needs to be an almost complete replacement of Israel with the Church and argued that this kind of separation is not found in Covenant Theology. He opined that the continuity for which Woudstra and Waltke argue is not the abandonment of the old promises, but the fulfillment of them. He further commented that in a system of continuity, the Church would

---

[12] Hans K. LaRondelle, *The Israel of God in Prophecy: Principles of Prophetic Interpretation* (Berrien Springs, MI: Andrews University Press, 1983), 101.

only replace Israel in the sense that a plant replaces the seed. Waltke bears this out. Conspicuously absent from the replacement he sets forth is the replacement of the promises of God. It is the supposition of the replacement of the promises of God on which MacArthur claims that Amillennialism fits better with Arminianism. MacArthur's argument will only fly if the Church is not a continuation of, but a complete replacement of Israel.

My response to all of this is as follows: I am open to the idea that many Amillennialists may have used words like replace and supersede in an unqualified way. I am open to the idea that some still do today. Nevertheless, this use of these words is different from the freight carried by Dispensational accusations of replacement theology and supersessionism. At any rate, I want to say that I am definitely with those mentioned by Woudstra who want to speak of a continuation and reformation of Israel rather than a simple replacement. The fact is that the key passage cited above (Matthew 21:43) is not speaking of the whole Jewish nation unqualifiedly, but of the nation as directed by its then present Jewish leadership. Often in the gospel accounts the references to "the Jews" are clearly references to this leadership.[13] In the case of Matthew 21:43, I think the focal point of Jesus' language is that he is going to replace the existing Jewish leadership with leaders of His own appointment (i.e., His Apostles). The reconstituted Israel, which begins first of all with the remnant of ethnic Jews according to the election of grace, will bring forth the fruits of the kingdom under this new leadership. This is where a distinction between corporate Israel and individual Israelites has value.

---

[13] In John's Gospel, for instance, the phrase, the Jews, is a reference to the Jewish leaders and not to the Jewish people as a whole (John 1:19; 7:13; 9:22).

CHAPTER SIX
The Israel of God

It should come as no surprise when I say one of the key differences between MacArthur and Amillennialists is our belief that the Church is (to borrow the much-debated and now famous language of Galatians 6:16) "the Israel of God." Later, we will ask if such an assertion truly requires a "spiritualizing" hermeneutic and whether it deserves the charge of spiritualizing or allegorizing the Scriptures. This hermeneutical issue is a clear second difference we have with MacArthur. Here, however, it is the fact that the Church is the Israel of God and not the explanation of this fact that is in view. In other words, in this chapter and the ones immediately to follow, I will affirm and attempt to prove what most Premillennialists, Amillennialists, and Postmillennialists historically have taken for granted–that the Church is the Israel of God.

In my book on eschatology, which is with some audacity entitled, *The End Times Made Simple*,[1] I spent a considerable amount of energy and spilled a lot of ink attempting to provide a balanced treatment of the relation of the Church and Israel. I labored to show both the unity of the Church and Israel and the superiority of the Church to Israel. Similarly, I also attempted to fulfill both of the missions mentioned in the previous paragraph: (1) show that the Church is the Israel of God and (2) demonstrate how that can be said without asserting that the New Testament supports a spiritualizing hermeneutic. Finally, I provided a summary of the vast New Testament evidence which affirms the Church as the Israel of God. Since that work is readily accessible, I am not going to review and expand all that evidentiary material in our present discussion.

---

[1] Samuel E. Waldron, *The End Times Made Simple* (Amityville, NY: Calvary Press, 2003).

Rather, I want to focus in on a few key passages and provide a somewhat more detailed treatment of them in light of the claims made by MacArthur in his manifesto. What are MacArthur's claims? The following quotation adequately represents them:

> The Bible calls God "The God of Israel" over 200 times--the God of Israel. There are over 2000 references to Israel in Scripture. Not one of them means anything but Israel. Not one of them, including Romans 9:6 and Galatians 6:16, which are the only two passages that Amillennialists go to, to try to convince us that these passages cancel out the other 2000. There is no difficulty in interpreting those as simply meaning Jews who were believers, "the Israel of God." Israel always means Israel; it never means anything but Israel. Seventy-three New Testament uses of Israel always mean Israel.

This is one of those outrageous statements which could be used to make MacArthur look and sound silly. I really want to avoid doing that. I want to give MacArthur credit for knowing that we actually go to about a "zillion" passages to prove the Church is the Israel of God–not just two. I don't want to take seriously the Arminian-sounding illogic MacArthur seems to use here. "*All* always means *all* and never means anything but *all*." To which the proper answer is, of course, "But what does *all* mean?" MacArthur does sound like that, doesn't he? "*Israel* always means *Israel* and never means anything but *Israel*." To which the proper answer is, "But what does *Israel* mean?"

I do not attribute such reasoning to MacArthur–even though it would be easy to do so. Yet, such statements are indeed "red meat" for the Premillennial faithful and need to be cooked for a while. Here is what I think he is saying–if we charitably broil the "red meat" found here. I will summarize it in several assertions: (1) Every scriptural reference to Israel is a reference to ethnic or national Israel. (2) The assertion that the Church is Israel is doubtful because it is supported only by two passages. In contrast, a multitude of passages clearly refer to ethnic Israel. (3) The two passages that are used to support the idea that the Church is the Israel of God can be easily interpreted in line with all the clear uses of Israel as ethnic or national Israel. Let me make three brief counter-observations in response to these assertions.

First, MacArthur appears to adopt a kind of *majority-rule* hermeneutic in his understanding of the term "Israel." In other words, he implies if the vast majority of biblical usages of a word carry a certain meaning, then we must assume that they all must carry this meaning. Now, in all charity, let me say that I assume MacArthur knows better than this and normally does better than this in his exegesis of Scripture. Nevertheless, his listeners are supposed to find the idea that two of the seventy-three New Testament occurrences of "Israel" might have a different meaning from the other seventy-one exceedingly doubtful or even impossible. But let us test that implication. Take the biblical word for heaven. It usually refers to the physical heavens where the birds fly and where the stars reside. But, in a minority of occurrences, heaven clearly refers to the heaven of God. Similarly, take the biblical word *sheol* as another example. It usually refers to the grave or what is physically below. But, in a minority of occurrences it clearly refers to what we call hell. Take also the biblical word for death. It usually and almost exclusively refers to physical death. Yet, in a very few cases (comparatively), it refers either to eternal death (the second death in the lake of fire–Revelation 2:11) or spiritual death (total depravity and inability in sin–Ephesians 2:1-3). Finally, take the Hebrew word *Elohim*, which occurs well over 2200 times in the Old Testament. *Elohim* almost always refers to either the true God or to false gods. Yet, there are a few famous cases in which it does not and cannot mean god. Rather, in those instances, it must mean a human ruler (Psalm 82:6) or mighty angel (Psalm 8:5). In light of this reality, there should be nothing particularly surprising (given the way the Bible uses words) if we were to discover that two of the 73 uses of Israel in the New Testament might actually refer to the Church.[2]

However, lest I be misunderstood, let me point out the obvious. It is not the position of Amillennialists that Israel always refers to the Church in the New Testament. We grant that sometimes and, indeed, in the vast majority of cases it does in fact refer to ethnic Israel. I pointed out in the previous chapter that a large number, and perhaps a majority of Amillennialists and Postmillennialists freely acknowledge a reference to ethnic Israel in Romans 11. Our position simply is (and only requires) that there is good and necessary reason

---

[2] Actually, I count sixty-eight uses of Israel and nine uses of Israelite in the New Testament, but I do not want to quibble.

to think in a small number of cases the Church is connoted by the term Israel.

Second, I acknowledge that Romans 9:6 and Galatians 6:16 are indeed the two classic passages which illustrate this way of using the term Israel. They are not the only passages, but they are the two classic texts. Nevertheless, I maintain there are a number of things reflected in other biblical usages of Israel which support the description of the Church as the new and true Israel of God.

Finally, MacArthur's argument ignores a simple fact. Those who hold the historic position that the Church is God's Israel argue their view not only from the use of Israel in Romans 9:6 and Galatians 6:16, but from the use of the biblical synonyms for Israel as well. It should be acknowledged (and most do acknowledge) that terms and phrases like Abraham's seed, the circumcision, the one olive tree, and Jew–to name only a few–are substantially synonymous or parallel with the term. If the Church is called Abraham's seed, described as the true circumcision, explained as the one olive tree, and referred to as the true Jews, it seems patently absurd to maintain that this is insignificant for the present discussion. It is simply wrong for MacArthur to ignore the use of the biblical synonyms for Israel when a major part of his adversaries' case is based precisely on the use of those synonyms. Furthermore, such indifference misrepresents the true breadth of the biblical evidence for viewing the Church as the Israel of God.

CHAPTER SEVEN
Galatians 6:16

As I read the debate between Dispensationalists and those they call Supersessionists, I confront a sense of near hopelessness in bringing out the true meaning of Galatians 6:16. The cause of this incipient despair is not that I think the text is unclear. It has been indisputably clear to me ever since I ran across it in college while re-examining the Dispensationalism upon which I had been nurtured from childhood. My "despair" is rather due to the creativity with which Dispensationalists have stubbornly defended the idea that the phrase "Israel of God" in the text cannot refer to the Church.

What can I add, then, to the volumes that have already been written on this text against Dispensationalism? Perhaps nothing. Yet, it stands written "the entrance of Thy words gives light." So, let me try again to make clear to my Dispensational brethren that the Israel of God *is* and *must be* a reference to the Church of Christ. Two things may help me in this task.

First, I want to avoid attacking a straw man. Much of what I have already written about MacArthur's millennial manifesto has been an extended and, I hope, kind and respectful objection to this very thing in MacArthur's message. He has successfully demolished a straw man in his message. But, he has not demolished the real Amillennial position. I don't want to be guilty of the same thing. Let me quote, therefore, from the website of someone whom I think represents the position of MacArthur and The Master's Seminary. Michael J. Vlach is a Professor of Theology at the Master's Seminary in Sun Valley, California. He is also the founder and president of TheologicalStudies.org, a cutting-edge website devoted to providing quality articles, news, and information related to Christian theology. Vlach specifically addresses the problem of Galatians 6:16 on his website:

Galatians 6:16 – Paul is referring to Christian Jews in his reference to the "Israel of God." Paul scolded the Judaizers who said circumcision was necessary for salvation, but he acknowledges those Jews in Galatia who had not followed the Judaizers in their error. These Christian Jews are the true "Israel of God." Ronald E. Diprose: "Galatians 6:16 is insufficient grounds on which to base an innovative theological concept such as understanding the Church to be the *new* and/or *true* Israel."[1]

This quotation is significant because Vlach, like MacArthur, cites Ronald Diprose in support of their so-called anti-Supersessionist position. Recall what MacArthur said in his message:

I suggest for your reading *Israel and the Church* by Ronald Diprose. We should have some in the bookstore. It first appeared in Italian. It was a Ph.D. dissertation. It has no connection to traditional Dispensationalism. It's a really fine work on replacement theology.

Vlach's association with The Master's Seminary and quotation of Diprose provides strong reason to think he is representing MacArthur's position regarding Galatians 6:16. At any rate, there is really no other position someone defending Vlach's view might take regarding this passage. So, I hope in citing Vlach's and Diprose's exegesis I will avoid attacking a straw man.

The second help to which I will appeal in order to make some progress on defining "the Israel of God" is the *context* of the passage in question. I adhere (and I expect everyone involved in this discussion adheres) to the idea that the true meaning of a word, phrase, or sentence is its meaning within the context it is made. In this sense *context is king* in biblical interpretation. It is context that must and does determine the specific meaning of a word. Out of the semantic range of a word, it is context that determines the precise nuance we attribute to a word or phrase in any given occurrence. The application of this principle to Galatians 6:16 is really quite

---

[1] Michael Vlach, "12 Reasons Why Supersessionism/Replacement Theology Is Not a Biblical Doctrine." This article may be accessed at http://www.theologicalstudies.citymax.com/page/page/4425336.htm. I accessed it May 25, 2007. The quotation is from Ronald E. Diprose, *Israel in the Development of Christian Thought* (Rome: Istituto Biblico Evangelico Italiano, 2000), 47.

straightforward. While we acknowledge that Israel might mean and in some contexts does mean the physical nation or ethnic people of Israel, the question is whether this is its meaning in Galatians 6:16.[2] For instance, I acknowledged in a previous chapter that the meaning of Israel in Romans 11 is, in fact, ethnic or national. However, the question remains whether this is its meaning here in Galatians 6:16. My answer to this question is *absolutely not*.

In Galatians 6:16, Israel does not refer exclusively to ethnic Jews, but to the entire Church of Christ.[3] It is the context that demands this assertion. Let me anticipate, however, the objection of Diprose cited by Vlach. Diprose writes, "Galatians 6:16 is insufficient grounds on which to base an innovative theological concept such as understanding the Church to be the *new* and/or *true* Israel." Diprose regards my understanding of "the Israel of God" as innovative. MacArthur even says that *only* Romans 9:6 and our current passage are cited as support for viewing this phrase as a reference to the Church. In what follows, I will show that such a reference is not solely based on Galatians 6:16. Nor is it solely based on Romans 9:6. Rather, it has a much broader basis both in the other uses of Israel in the New Testament and in the fact that various synonyms for Israel are used to refer to the Church. Thus, though I only examine the immediate context of Galatians 6:16 in my interpretation below, I am confident that my interpretation will be supported by the broader context of the New Testament itself.

To begin with, let me state my interpretive approach to Galatians 6:16. The phrase in question, "Israel of God", occurs almost at the end of the letter in verse 16. Also, there seems to be nothing of significance for our question in the remainder of the letter following the use of this phrase. Consequently, my strategy for interpreting this key phrase will be to read backward through the letter. In so

---

[2] I am not so sure that the phrase, Israel of God, could refer to the ethnic people of Israel. This phrase occurs only here in the NT and LXX. My point is only that Israel may refer and in some contexts does refer to Israel ethnically.

[3] Originally, I took it for granted that no one would dispute that the phrase, "and upon the Israel of God," may be understood epexegetically or appositionally and need not be understood as adding another group to those previously described as *as many as* "those who will walk by this rule." A lengthy correspondence ensued, however, about exactly this point. Hence, on this point see the excursus at the end of this chapter.

doing, we will see how both the immediate and remote context of the letter sheds light on what Paul means by "the Israel of God."

When we employ this strategy of reading the epistle backward, a startling observation leaps to the forefront. In the immediately preceding context of Galatians 6:16, Paul is engaged in a polemic against those who were compelling the Galatians to be circumcised (Galatians 6:12). Paul pursues this polemic by affirming that those who do this do not even keep the law themselves (Galatians 6:13). He then asserts the true boast of the Christian is the crucifixion of Christ, not the circumcision of his flesh (Galatians 6:14). Following this, Paul emphatically declares that in Christ Jesus neither circumcision nor uncircumcision matters, but a new creation (Galatians 6:15). Now, in this context, would it not be startling, to say the least, for Paul to finish his polemic by referring to a sub-group of Christians who are distinguished precisely by their circumcision? Think of it. Paul has just said that circumcision means nothing in Christ. But now, according to the Dispensational interpretation, *in the very next verse*, Paul supposedly distinguishes between Jewish and Gentile Christians by exclusively awarding to Jewish Christians the honorable title, "Israel of God." And he does this solely on the basis of their circumcision in contrast with the Gentile Christians' uncircumcision. This would be a startling and, indeed, exceedingly unnatural thing for Paul to do–especially in this context. Furthermore, we must not fail to notice the parallel relationship between the phrases "new creation" and "Israel of God." The Church is described as a new creation.[4] It is the new creation–not circumcision or uncircumcision–that makes a man a member of the Israel of God. So, to make physical circumcision a necessary prerequisite for membership in the Israel of God flies in the face of the nearest context.

---

[4] One correspondent astutely noted that "a new creation" is not precisely a reference to the Church, but in context a reference to what matters in Christ Jesus, that is, what makes an individual saved and, thus, a member of the people of God. The new creation in Galatians 6:15, in other words, refers to the work of God in the individual and not strictly to the Church corporately. True enough! I have moved from the individual to the corporate in my comments. If a new creation makes an individual man saved and a member of the people of God, then it seems a simple, necessary, and straightforward deduction to conclude that the Church as a whole is a new creation.

As we continue to read backward through the epistle, Galatians 5:1-12 reminds us that the polemic against the circumcisers permeates the entire letter to this mainly Gentile church. A few sample statements from the passage will demonstrate this point:

> Galatians 5:2 Behold I, Paul, say to you that if you receive circumcision, Christ will be of no benefit to you.

> Galatians 5:3 And I testify again to every man who receives circumcision, that he is under obligation to keep the whole Law.

> Galatians 5:6 For in Christ Jesus neither circumcision nor uncircumcision means anything, but faith working through love.

> Galatians 5:11 But I, brethren, if I still preach circumcision, why am I still persecuted? Then the stumbling block of the cross has been abolished.

What is the relevance of these verses to Galatians 6:16? First, notice the parallel between 5:6 and 6:15. Once again, the complete meaninglessness of physical circumcision with regard to Christ Jesus is emphatically asserted. It is faith working through love, rather than circumcision, which marks the recipients of God's covenant blessings in Christ. Second, and also noteworthy in the context of 5:1-12, is Paul's positive rejection of receiving circumcision. The reception of circumcision in the context of Galatians means that *Christ will be of no benefit to you*. Of course, in other contexts Paul could take one such as Timothy and circumcise him. But, in the Galatian context, it was an entirely different matter. And, at the risk of pointing out the obvious, Galatians 6:16 is not in another context. Therefore, in this context, to exclusively attribute the phrase "Israel of God" to Jewish Christians is to imply that only the reception of circumcision would make a Christian a member of the Israel of God. Again, this is contrary to the entire thrust of Paul's argument.

In reality there are only two possibilities available for the Dispensationalist position. Either it is significant to be a member of the Israel of God, or it is insignificant. If it is insignificant, why does Paul bother to mention it? Why does Paul ascribe such an honorable title to Jewish Christians in contrast to Gentile Christians if such membership is insignificant? Yet, if it is significant to be a part of the Israel of God, we are left with a startling conclusion. At the very end of his letter, Paul would be implicitly encouraging physical circumcision. For, on the Dispensationalist interpretation, one cannot be a member of the Israel of God without circumcision. It is impossible to think that Paul would do this in *of all places* Galatians.

As we continue to read back through Galatians, we encounter Galatians 4:21-31. As a result, we encounter even more problems for the Dispensational interpretation. In Galatians 4:28, Paul describes the Gentile Galatians as children of promise (a fact quite significant for the interpretation of Romans 9:6, as we will see). He also makes the nature of the promise clear. The promise in view is the covenantal promise to the Jerusalem above which is both free and the mother of all Christians including the Galatian, Gentile ones (Galatians 4:25-26). Now, it is not part of our purpose to discuss the nature of Paul's hermeneutic at this point. However, one thing is clearly pertinent. To exclude Gentile Christians from the Israel of God in 6:16 is parallel to excluding them from the children of promise in 4:28. Dispensationalists, in fact, do this very thing in Romans 9:6. Yet, Paul makes it crystal clear in this text. It is impossible to avoid the conclusion that Gentile Christians are entitled to the description "children of promise" and the sons of the true Jerusalem. Paul knows nothing of the kind of distinction Dispensationalism attributes to the phrase "Israel of God."

Moving further, our journey back through Galatians brings us to Galatians 3:29. With this text, we find the assertion "all who belong to Christ are the seed of Abraham." In this context, Paul emphasizes that distinctions between Jew and Greek mean nothing with regard to this matter (3:28). There can be no doubt (and, indeed, many Dispensationalists do not deny) the seed of Abraham includes all Christians. This may not seem inconsistent or strange to them, but it does to us. Must we really say that Gentile Christians are not part of the Israel of God, but they are part of the seed of Abraham? Upon what strange Dispensational distinction between Abraham and Israel is such a contrast grounded? Beyond this, we encounter a similar assertion in Galatians 3:7, where Gentile Christians are called "the sons of Abraham." Again we ask: Upon what basis must we interpret a phrase like "the Israel of God" with strict and wooden literality? Yet, we are to believe that we need not interpret phrases like sons of Abraham or seed of Abraham with a similar literalistic hermeneutic. This is all the more unaccountable and arbitrary in light of the constant equivalency in the Old Testament between the seed of Abraham, the seed of Isaac, and national Israel. Let me also add the first two chapters of Galatians are consistent with all this as well. For, it is in the first two chapters we see the beginning of Paul's polemic against the circumcisers.

In light of the context of Galatians 6:16 in the letter as a whole, there is every reason to reject the Dispensational understanding of the phrase "the Israel of God." Instead, we should regard it as parallel in meaning to "sons of Abraham," "seed of Abraham," "children of promise," and being sons of the Jerusalem above. In none of these phrases is there any question that Gentile Christians are included. There ought to be no such question with regard to the Israel of God in Galatians 6:16. The only reason for MacArthur and his Dispensational brethren to exclude the Gentiles from the Israel of God in 6:16 is the doctrinal constraints of the Dispensational system–not the exegetical constraints of Scripture. The entire letter is a polemic against the Judaizers who insisted on the necessity of physical circumcision for authentic Christianity and true membership in the people of God. Consequently, when Dispensationalists argue that physical circumcision is necessary to membership in the Israel of God they are out of step with the argument of the entire epistle.

Excursus: On the Meaning of Kai in the Phrase "and [kai] upon the Israel of God" in Galatians 6:16

There are two possible ways (in the abstract) to understand the phrase in question. First, it may be translated, "and upon the Israel of God." This translation suggests and supports the Dispensational understanding of the text. The support stems from the affirmation that there are two distinct groups upon which Paul pronounces his blessing: (1) those who walk according to the rule *and* (2) the Israel of God. This translation, then, distinguishes the Israel of God (group 2) from those who walk according to the rule (group 1). The second way of translating the phrase reads, "even (or "to be specific") upon the Israel of God." This way of translating the *kai* [and] does not distinguish the Israel of God from those who walk according to the rule. Rather, it identifies them with those who walk according to the rule. Thus, this translation supports the idea that only one group is in view and this group is the Christian Church here identified as the Israel of God.

As I noted above, I originally assumed that there would be no dispute about this second meaning of *kai* and the legitimacy of my understanding of the text. I thought everyone, while not necessarily agreeing with my interpretation, would agree that *kai* could be understood in this way without being inconsistent with its meaning and use in the New Testament. In other words, I thought everyone would grant the meaning of the Greek conjunction *kai* was broad enough to allow without question that this phrase could be translated, "even (or "to be specific") upon the Israel of God." I sincerely did not think anyone would challenge the plausibility of an appositional or epexegetical force for *kai* in this phrase. Among my correspondents, there ensued such an extensive debate on this subject that I was convinced of the importance of an excursus on the meaning of *kai* in Galatians 6:16.

In this excursus I want to do two things. First, I want to demonstrate that the epexegetical or appositional meaning of *kai* in this phrase is not undermined by the fact that such usage of *kai* is comparatively rare. Second, I want to show that the internal meaning of the text in which the phrase occurs (Galatians 6:16) demands that we take *kai* with an epexegetical or appositional force.

To begin with, let me demonstrate how the epexegetical or appositional meaning of *kai* in this phrase is not undermined by the fact that such usage of *kai* is comparatively rare. One of my correspondents questioned my exegesis of *kai* in Galatians 6:16. He asserted that I was assuming "an extremely rare use of the Greek conjunction *kai*." I was rather surprised by this assertion and so were a number of other correspondents. My response is that while the epexegetical or appositional use of *kai* is comparatively rare (not extremely rare as my correspondent suggested) it is nevertheless well attested in the standard lexicons. The standard lexicon, BAG, lists the meanings of *kai* under two headings. Both headings list as a standard definition a meaning which sustains the interpretation I have given to the phrase in question.[5] Under the first heading it lists

---

[5] Walter Bauer, *A Greek-English Lexicon of the New Testament and Other Early Christian Literature*, trans. and adapted by William F. Arndt and F. Wilbur Gingrich (Chicago: The University of Chicago Press, 1957), 392-394.

and supports an explicative meaning and comment: "a word or clause is connected by means of *kai* w. another word or clause, for the purpose of explaining what goes before." They give the various meanings "and so, that is and namely." This is a possible meaning on the covenantal approach to Galatians 6:16, "*namely*, or, *that is* the Israel of God." Under the second heading they list the ascensive meaning, "even." Again, this use of *kai* coheres with the covenantal interpretation and may be translated, "*even* upon the Israel of God." I believe, therefore, the objection that the usage I assume is extremely rare misrepresents the facts of the case. This use may be infrequent and even in some sense comparatively rare, but it is well-attested. The description 'extremely rare' undermines this fact. In my opinion one who objects to the covenantal interpretation of Galatians 6:16 on this ground is really allowing the false, majority-rule hermeneutic to control his exegesis. As I mentioned earlier, the meaning of angel or human ruler for *elohim* (which almost always means God or god) may be even rarer in terms of sheer percentages than the explicative and ascensive uses of *kai*. Nevertheless, there is no question that in some passages these meanings are indisputable (Psalms 8:5; 82:6).[6]

Second, let me show that the internal meaning of the text in which the phrase occurs (Galatians 6:16) demands that we take *kai* to have an epexegetical or appositional force. Here I ask the reader to note the occurrence of the word ὅσος, meaning as many as–no more and no less–in the Greek phrase: ὅσοι τῷ κανόνι τούτῳ στοιχήσουσιν (lit. "as many as will walk by this rule"). Its occurrence rather suggests the appositional or epexegetical explanation. If Paul has already wished that *as many as* walk according to this rule should have peace and mercy, why is there a need to add an additional group already included in the initial blessing? It makes more sense to think Paul is clarifying that those who walk by this rule are *the Israel of God*.

Let me expand upon and clarify what I have just written. I am affirming that the internal grammar of Galatians 6:16 demands or at least strongly suggests the meaning of "namely" or "even" for *kai*. Both ways of reading the text (*and* upon the Israel of God or *even* upon the Israel of God) are perfectly legitimate from a grammatical

---

[6] I am indebted to one of my correspondents for this illustration of the danger of the majority-rule hermeneutic.

viewpoint. Both, in other words, in the abstract are possible readings of the Greek. But, there is an internal indication in the text itself which points to the rightness of the covenantal view. The first part of the text contains a Greek word that is not clearly translated in the NASB. It is a Greek word that means *as many as*. If you have a KJV, NKJV, or ESV, you will see this word more clearly translated. The old KJV, for instance, says, "And as many as walk according to this rule, peace be on them, and mercy, and upon the Israel of God." So why is this important? Well, if Paul has already pronounced the blessing on as many as walk according to this rule, then why does he need to say–as the Dispensational interpretation has him say–"and also upon the Israel of God"? This interpretation of the text, in other words, makes the last words of the text superfluous. Christian Jews already walk according to the rule as true Christians. So, there is no need to add "also upon the Israel of God."

After engaging in this consideration of Galatians 6:16 and correspondence about it, I was gratified to discover that O. Palmer Robertson concurred with the view that the grammar of the text actually supports and demands the epexegetical meaning of *kai* here defended. He remarks:

> The only explanation of Paul's phrase "the Israel of God" that satisfies the context as well as the grammar of the passage also begins by understanding the Greek conjunction *kai* as epexegetical of "all those who walk according to this canon." [7]

In closing, then, the epexegetical meaning is not only admissible, but is the most satisfactory option given the internal meaning of the passage. Once again, the Dispensationalist must make a distinction within the text that the text itself does not require.

---

[7] Robertson, *The Israel of God*, 43.

CHAPTER EIGHT
Romans 9:6

In this examination of Romans 9:6, I want to use the same two strategies I mentioned with regard to Galatians 6:16. First, I want to avoid attacking a straw man. Next, I want to make sure that I am guided by context in my interpretation of this key passage.

In order to avoid attacking a straw man, let me again quote Vlach's website as representative of MacArthur's position:

> Romans 9:6 – Believing Jews are those who are the true spiritual Israel. As William Sanday and Arthur C. Headlam state: "But St. Paul does not mean here to distinguish a spiritual Israel (i.e. the Christian Church) from the fleshly Israel, but to state that the promises made to Israel might be fulfilled even if some of his descendants were shut out from them. What he states is that not all the physical descendants of Jacob are necessarily inheritors of the Divine promises implied in the sacred name Israel."[1]

This comment is supported by the following footnote:

> William Sanday and Arthur C. Headlam, *The Epistle to the Romans*, ICC (New York: Charles Scribner's Sons, 1923), 240. See also Douglas Moo, *The Epistle to the Romans*, NICNT (Grand Rapids: Eerdmans, 1996), 574. About Rom 9:6, Gutbrod writes, **"We are not told here that Gentile Christians are the true Israel**. The distinction at R. 9:6 does not go beyond what is presupposed at Jn. 1:47. . . ." Walter Gutbrod, "'Israhl, k. t. l.," in

---

[1] Michael Vlach, "12 Reasons Why Supersessionism/Replacement Theology Is Not a Biblical Doctrine." This article may be accessed at http://www.theologicalstudies.citymax.com/page/page/4425336.htm. I accessed it May 25, 2007.

Theological Dictionary of the New Testament, vol. 3, ed. Gerhard
Kittel (Grand Rapids: Eerdmans, 1965), 387 [emphasis added].[2]

As with Galatians 6:16, we once again see the intentional exclusion
of the Gentiles from the Israel of God.

Next, by utilizing context to understand this key passage, it is
my concern to point out four observations about the assertion of
Romans 9:6. In order to accomplish this, we will look at what I will
call the immediate context, the near context, the further context in
Romans, and the wider New Testament context of this passage. So,
to begin with, let me cite this passage with some of its immediate
context:

> [1] I am telling the truth in Christ, I am not lying, my conscience
> testifies with me in the Holy Spirit, [2] that I have great sorrow and
> unceasing grief in my heart. [3] For I could wish that I myself were
> accursed, *separated* from Christ for the sake of my brethren, my
> kinsmen according to the flesh, [4] who are Israelites, to whom
> belongs the adoption as sons, and the glory and the covenants and
> the giving of the Law and the *temple* service and the promises, [5]
> whose are the fathers, and from whom is the Christ according to
> the flesh, who is over all, God blessed forever. Amen. [6] But *it is*
> not as though the word of God has failed. For they are not all
> Israel who are *descended* from Israel; [7] nor are they all children
> because they are Abraham's descendants, but: "THROUGH
> ISAAC YOUR DESCENDANTS WILL BE NAMED." [8] That is,
> it is not the children of the flesh who are children of God, but the
> children of the promise are regarded as descendants.

The Immediate Context

The point of Paul in this passage is clear. Paul is explaining an
obstacle to the acceptance of the gospel of Christ. The obstacle in
view concerns the fact that the mass of the ancient covenant people
of Israel, to whom the promises were made, have rejected the

---

[2] Michael Vlach, "12 Reasons Why Supersessionism/Replacement Theology
Is Not a Biblical Doctrine." This article may be accessed at
http://www.theologicalstudies.citymax.com/page/page/4425336.htm. I accessed it
May 25, 2007.

gospel. How could this happen? How especially could this happen consistent with the truthfulness of the gospel?

Paul maintains a uniform response to this problem here and throughout Romans 9-11. From the beginning of God's dealings with the nation of Israel the promises have always been to the believing remnant of the Jewish nation and not to every fleshly descendant of Abraham or Israel. In the immediate context, Paul proves this by two Old Testament citations and examples: the contrast between Isaac and Ishmael and the contrast between Jacob and Esau. Later he will argue that his own example as a believer in the gospel of Christ and the account of Elijah in the Old Testament also prove that God has not abandoned His promises to Israel. Rather, He is fulfilling them to the elect remnant (Romans 11:1-6).

It must, therefore, be acknowledged that it is not Paul's *main* point here to prove that Gentiles are now included in God's Israel. To this extent Vlach and MacArthur are right. Paul's *main* point is not that Gentile Christians are part of God's Israel, but rather that there is a remnant among ethnic Israelites in which God's promise is fulfilled. Yet, this is not quite the same as proving that the inclusion of Gentile Christians in God's Israel is not implied. Even though something may not be the main point of a given statement, it may still be implied. There are two things in the immediate context which actually provide a foundation for such an implication. First, there is clearly an emphasis on God's personal election of Isaac and Jacob for salvation (9:11-13). This at least opens the way for the idea that Gentiles elected to salvation are included in the Israel of God. Second, there is an emphasis in the immediate context on the supernatural birth of the true seed of Abraham (9:7-9). It is not fleshly ability, but God's mighty promise that brings forth the true seed of Abraham. This brings to mind a similar statement in John 1:11-13:

> [11] He came to His own, and those who were His own did not receive Him. [12] But as many as received Him, to them He gave the right to become children of God, *even* to those who believe in His name, [13] who were born, not of blood nor of the will of the flesh nor of the will of man, but of God.

God's children are born of the Spirit–not of the flesh–and *as many as* receive Christ are born in this way. They are God's children and the true seed of Abraham. Thus, both the emphasis on personal election to salvation and a supernatural birth create a foundation through which Gentiles might be thought of as included in God's Israel.

The Near Context

By *the near context*, I am referring to the statements later in Romans 9 that explicitly include Gentiles in the people of God. Consider Romans 9:23-26:

> [23] And *He did so* to make known the riches of His glory upon vessels of mercy, which He prepared beforehand for glory, [24] *even* us, whom He also called, not from among Jews only, but also from among Gentiles. [25] As He says also in Hosea, "I WILL CALL THOSE WHO WERE NOT MY PEOPLE, 'MY PEOPLE,' AND HER WHO WAS NOT BELOVED, 'BELOVED.'" [26] "AND IT SHALL BE THAT IN THE PLACE WHERE IT WAS SAID TO THEM, 'YOU ARE NOT MY PEOPLE,' THERE THEY SHALL BE CALLED SONS OF THE LIVING GOD."

This passage affirms that Gentiles are now included in the people of God with elect Israelites. Now, contemporary Dispensationalists like to say that Gentiles share in the blessings of the covenant with Israel without actually becoming a part of Israel. Consider Vlach's statements on this subject:

> Ephesians 2:11–22 shows that Gentiles who used to be far from God have now been brought near God because of Christ. Thus, the soteriological status of believing Gentiles has changed. They now share with Israel in Israel's covenants and promises but they do not become Israel.

> Rom 11:17–24 stresses that Gentiles are now related to the promises of God. Thus, there is a soteriological unity between believing Jews and Gentiles. But it does not indicate that the church is now the true Israel. There is a difference between saying that Gentiles participate with Israel in Israel's covenants and claiming that believing Gentiles become Israel. Gentiles are partakers of the covenants not taker-overs. This passage does not

rule out a future role for national Israel or indicate that the church is now Israel. [3]

This passage strongly suggests that such distinctions are fallacious. It suggests that elect Gentiles are now included in what Hosea calls the people of God and counted among the sons of the living God. Elect Gentiles are not a Gentile auxiliary to the people of God. They are themselves part of the people of God. The name of that people (among many other names) is *Israel*.

The Further Context in Romans

Here I am referencing the statements of Romans 2:25-29 which confirm the conclusions just mentioned above:

[25] For indeed circumcision is of value if you practice the Law; but if you are a transgressor of the Law, your circumcision has become uncircumcision. [26] So if the uncircumcised man keeps the requirements of the Law, will not his uncircumcision be regarded as circumcision? [27] And he who is physically uncircumcised, if he keeps the Law, will he not judge you who though having the letter *of the Law* and circumcision are a transgressor of the Law? [28] For he is not a Jew who is one outwardly, nor is circumcision that which is outward in the flesh. [29] But he is a Jew who is one inwardly; and circumcision is that which is of the heart, by the Spirit, not by the letter; and his praise is not from men, but from God.

Paul is not satisfied merely to say that physical circumcision becomes equivalent to physical uncircumcision if one does not faithfully practice the law. No, he goes further than this. The reverse is also true. In verse 26, Paul asks if the uncircumcised man who keeps the requirements of the law will not be regarded as circumcised. The answer clearly assumed is yes. Paul then goes on to assert the identical viewpoint that we found repeatedly in Galatians 6:16 and 5:6. There is the complete dismissal of physical

---

[3] Michael Vlach, "12 Reasons Why Supersessionism/Replacement Theology Is Not a Biblical Doctrine." This article may be accessed at http://www.theologicalstudies.citymax.com/page/page/4425336.htm. I accessed it May 25, 2007.

circumcision. True circumcision and, Paul adds, true Jewish-ness are entirely a matter of the heart. Being born of the Spirit does not merely constitute one as an auxiliary to the true circumcision or to the Jewish nation. It constitutes one as actually being a part of the true circumcision and the true Jewish nation.

The Wider Context in the New Testament

Here we return to Galatians 4:28 and its immediate context (Galatians 4:26-29):

> [26] But the Jerusalem above is free; she is our mother. [27] For it is written, "REJOICE, BARREN WOMAN WHO DOES NOT BEAR; BREAK FORTH AND SHOUT, YOU WHO ARE NOT IN LABOR; FOR MORE NUMEROUS ARE THE CHILDREN OF THE DESOLATE THAN OF THE ONE WHO HAS A HUSBAND." [28] And you brethren, like Isaac, are children of promise. [29] But as at that time he who was born according to the flesh persecuted him *who was born* according to the Spirit, so it is now also.

Galatians 4:28, in language almost identical to Romans 9:7, identifies the Gentile Galatian Christians as "the children of promise." Both the Greek word for promise and the Greek word for children used in Romans 9:7 are used in Galatians 4:28. In Romans 9:7, the true Israel is identified as the children of promise. We have then, in Galatians, an explicit rebuttal of the Dispensational idea that Gentiles are not part of the true Israel. The true Israel is composed of the children of promise. The children of promise include Gentile Christians.

Conclusion

Consider the predicament in which these texts place Vlach, MacArthur, and contemporary Dispensationalists. They must maintain that language like "the children of promise," "My people," "the sons of the living God," and "the circumcision" all includes Gentile Christians, while "Israel" does not. Israel is defined as the children of promise. Yet, we are to believe that Israel, unlike the children of promise, does not include Gentiles. Israel is synonymous with the circumcision (Jeremiah 9:25-26; Ephesians 2:11-12; Philippians 3:5). But, though the true circumcision includes Gentiles, Israel does not. Israel was the son of God. Although the sons of the living God now include Gentiles, Israel does not. Gentiles are part of God's people and one name for God's people was Israel. Yet, though God's people include Gentiles, Israel may not and does not. Such distinctions, let me say it as politely as possible, are exegetical impossibilities.

CHAPTER NINE
1 Corinthians 10:18 and 12:2

In his message, John MacArthur argues that Amillennialists only have two passages (beside Romans 11:26) to which they appeal to show the Church is Israel. I have argued that this approach ignores the synonyms for Israel used throughout the New Testament to describe the Church. I have also argued that Galatians 6:16 and Romans 9:6 both affirm more or less explicitly that the Church is Israel. Now I want to go further and argue that MacArthur also ignores several other passages which either imply or actually assert that the Christian Church is God's Israel.

Before I come to the major and most explicit passage, I want to point to two additional passages which, in light of the rest of the New Testament, strongly suggest the Church is God's Israel. They are passages that are often overlooked, but whose implications are from my view unmistakable. One of these passages uses the term, Israel, and one uses the opposite term, Gentile. Both passages are found in Paul's first epistle to the Corinthians.

First, let us examine 1 Corinthians 10:18. The King James Version provides a literal translation of this verse, "Behold Israel after the flesh." It should be noted that this translation is greatly preferable to that of the NASB, "Look at the nation Israel," which disguises and obscures the Greek words "after the flesh." The NIV also disguises this language and reads *"Consider the people of Israel."* The ASV and NKJV follow the more literal translation of the KJV. Why is this so important? Students of Paul will recognize in the prepositional phrase "after the flesh"–*kata sarka*–the familiar Pauline contrast between those things that are after the flesh and those things that are after the Spirit (see also Romans 1:3-4; 2:28-29; 7:5-6, 14; 8:4, 5, 6, 9, 12-13; 1 Corinthians 3:1; Galatians 3:3; 4:29;

5:16, 17; 6:8; Philippians 3:3-4; and 1 Timothy 3:1).What does this mean? When Paul speaks of "Israel after the flesh," he directly implies that there is an "Israel after the Spirit." As we have seen, this cannot be a reference merely to Christian Jews, but must be a reference to all those born not of the flesh, but of the Spirit (John 1:11-13). It must, in other words, be a reference to the Church of Christ. Thus, in 1 Corinthians 10:18, we have a use of Israel that implicitly, but very suggestively, refers to the Christian Church.

Admittedly, the second passage I have in mind (1 Corinthians 12:2) does not use the term Israel. It does, however, use the antonym or opposite of Israel, i.e. the term "Gentiles." Throughout the New Testament, Israel is frequently contrasted with the Gentile nations. Again, however, the true implications of 1 Corinthians 12:2 are disguised by unhelpful paraphrases of its language in some translations. The NASB reads as follows, "You know that when you were pagans, *you were* led astray to the mute idols, however you were led." The NIV also follows this translation at the key point. The ASV and the NKJV, however, adopt a more literal translation of the Greek. The ASV translates, "Ye know that when ye were Gentiles *ye were* led away unto those dumb idols, howsoever ye might be led." The common Greek word for Gentiles is used here. It is not necessary to dispute whether the translation (i.e., "pagans") brings out an aspect of the meaning of the word. We need only understand that it misses the connection of this nuance with the Jewish attitude toward those who were "sinners of the Gentiles" (Galatians 2:15). But, the key point is that Paul places their Gentile-ness in the past and implies that they are no longer Gentiles. He says, "You know that when you *were* pagans (Gentiles), you *were led* astray to the mute idols, however you *were led.*" The Christians at Corinth are no longer Gentiles. In the language of this passage, they are not even Gentile Christians. In fact, they are not from one important perspective Gentiles at all. Rather, they are members of God's New Israel.

Now, I admit that passages like 1 Corinthians 10:18 and 12:2 are more likely to encourage the friends of my position than to convince its opponents the Church is the Israel of God. Nevertheless, it is my hope that the sheer accumulation of evidence and the ring of truth in Scripture may play a part in cracking the walls of someone's Dispensational understanding. Furthermore, I am aware that

Dispensationalists are likely to reply – especially to my use of 1 Corinthians 12:2 – that there are no longer just two kinds of people in the world. Rather, there are three. They will cite 1 Corinthians 10:32, "Give none offence, neither to the Jews, nor to the Gentiles, nor to the church of God" as proof. So, they will argue that Paul does not imply that the former Gentiles are now Israelites, but that they are a new kind of man–"the one new man"–known as the Church. Vlach, for instance, argues, "Believing Gentiles cannot be incorporated into Israel because Paul says they are now part of a new structure–the new man."[1] From one point of view this cannot be denied. Of course, the Church has passed beyond the old divisions between ethnic Jews and ethnic Gentiles. Amillennialists do not deny that the term "Israel" here and in many places refers to the ethnic people of Israel. Neither are we saying the Church is Old Israel. What we are saying is that the Church is New Israel and *in this sense* a new man or humanity.

I am not persuaded, however, that Vlach's argument really satisfies the implication of Paul's statement in 1 Corinthians 12:2 that the Corinthians believers were no longer Gentiles. Vlach, MacArthur, and other Dispensationalists insist on the continuing importance of the Israel/Gentile distinction even among Christians. Recall their interpretation of "the Israel of God" in Galatians 6:16. Yet, if they are correct, Paul ought not to have said that the Corinthian believers were no longer Gentiles. Rather, he should have said that they were Christian Gentiles.

Similarly, I am not persuaded that this approach answers at all the implicit contrast between "Israel after the flesh" and *Israel after the Spirit* in 1 Corinthians 10:18. The contrast between flesh and Spirit in Paul is dual, not trine. There is only "Israel after the flesh" and *Israel after the Spirit*. There is no third group. In other words, *Israel after the Spirit* is and must be the Church of God to whom we are to give no offense (1 Corinthians 10:32).

---

[1] Michael Vlach, "12 Reasons Why Supersessionism/Replacement Theology Is Not a Biblical Doctrine," The article may be accessed at http://www.theologicalstudies.citymax.com/page/page/4425336.htm. I accessed it May 25, 2007.

CHAPTER TEN
Ephesians 2:12-19

I have granted and hereby again grant that 1 Corinthians 10:18 and 12:2 suggestively imply, rather than overtly and explicitly state, the Church is God's New Israel. Nevertheless, 1 Corinthians 10:18 at least counts in my view as one more usage of Israel to refer to the Church. More importantly, however, I am convinced that Vlach's argument utterly fails when it is applied to Ephesians 2:12-19. This passage constitutes the most explicit and crucial passage for assessing the Dispensational denial that the Church is the Israel of God.

The use of Israel in Ephesians 2:12 cannot be regarded as anything but an explicit reference to the Church. I know this is a strong statement. I must now support it. But first, I think it will be helpful to quote the passage beginning with verse 11:

> [11] Therefore remember that formerly you, the Gentiles in the flesh, who are called "Uncircumcision" by the so-called "Circumcision," *which is* performed in the flesh by human hands - [12] *remember* that you were at that time separate from Christ, excluded from the commonwealth of Israel, and strangers to the covenants of promise, having no hope and without God in the world. [13] But now in Christ Jesus you who formerly were far off have been brought near by the blood of Christ. [14] For He Himself is our peace, who made both *groups into* one and broke down the barrier of the dividing wall, [15] by abolishing in His flesh the enmity, *which is* the Law of commandments *contained* in ordinances, so that in Himself He might make the two into one new man, *thus* establishing peace, [16] and might reconcile them both in one body to God through the cross, by it having put to death the enmity. [17] AND HE CAME AND PREACHED PEACE TO YOU WHO WERE FAR AWAY, AND PEACE TO THOSE WHO WERE

NEAR; [18] for through Him we both have our access in one Spirit
to the Father. [19] So then you are no longer strangers and aliens, but
you are fellow citizens with the saints, and are of God's household.

Verse 11 begins with a number of comments about fleshly
circumcision which must not be overlooked in our examination of
the passage. Paul describes his readers in verse 11 as "Gentiles in
the flesh." This description is significant in two respects. First, Paul
clearly is concerned in this passage with the contrast between ethnic
Gentiles and ethnic Israel. Second, this phrase strongly implies that
Paul regards the believing Gentiles he is addressing as only Gentiles
"in the flesh." That is to say, the phrase "in the flesh" suggests that
after (or with reference to) the Spirit they were not Gentiles but Jews
or Israelites (recall 1 Corinthians 10:18 and 12:2). This suggestion is
further strengthened by the way Paul emphasizes that unbelieving
ethnic Israelites are only "called" or "named" circumcision, just as
they only "call" or "name" the believing Gentiles "uncircumcision."
There is no reason to quibble with the NASB's translation "so-
called" in verse 11. This is Paul's precise meaning. The whole verse,
in other words, implies that to judge someone's "Jewish-ness" or
"Gentile-ness" by physical circumcision is a mistake. Also, by
implication, believing Gentiles are the true circumcision
(Philippians 3:3; Romans 2:25-29) and unbelieving Jews may not be
the circumcision or Israel (spiritually speaking) at all.

As we move on to verse 12, we find the first half of a temporal
contrast which concludes in verse 13. In the past, Gentiles were
separated or excluded from five things mentioned in verse 12,
"separate from Christ, excluded from the commonwealth of Israel,
and strangers to the covenants of promise, having no hope and
without God in the world." They were without Christ, the
commonwealth of Israel, the covenants of promise, hope, and God.
Verse 13 states the second half of this temporal contrast. In the
present time, believing Gentiles are brought near to or made
participants in all the things from which they were formerly
excluded, "But now in Christ Jesus you who formerly were far off
have been brought near by the blood of Christ." It should not need to
be said, though it is frequently overlooked by Dispensationalists,
that verse 13's assertion must be understood in accordance with the
context set by verse 12. In other words, when verse 13 says the
believing Gentiles are brought near, the question is raised, near to

what? This question cannot and must not be answered out of thin air or out of our imaginations. It must be answered on the basis of the context. When the context is consulted, it supplies an obvious answer. The Gentiles are made near to all the things from which they were formerly excluded. And what are those things? According to verse 12, they were excluded from Christ, the commonwealth of Israel, the covenants of promise, hope, and God. I hope the significance of this conclusion is obvious. Just in case it is not, let me spell it out. Gentiles are made near to, or in other words, made participants in "the commonwealth of Israel." Now if they are made near to–participants in–the commonwealth of Israel, this means (it seems clear to me) that they are *Israelites*. Just as Americans are citizens of America, so also Israelites are citizens of Israel.

Paul continues to build on this unity in verses 14-18. Notice the emphasis on the new oneness between believing Gentiles and believing Israelites. The dividing wall has been broken down. In the Church of Christ there is "one new man." The *one* flesh of Christ was broken to reconcile us on the *one* cross of Christ. Consequently, there is *one* body of Christ.

The culmination of Paul's argument, which he began in verse 12, is found in verse 19. The language used in verse 19 is reminiscent of the language and concepts in verse 12 that referred to the commonwealth of Israel. The premier reminiscence is found in the phrase "fellow citizens with the saints." How does this phrase echo elements found in verse 12? Note that "the commonwealth of Israel" in verse 12 is τῆς πολιτείας τοῦ Ἰσραὴλ in the Greek text. In verse 19, the reminiscent element is seen in the use of the same root found in the word translated "commonwealth" (πολιτείας). This root appears in the phrase translated "fellow-citizens" (συμπολῖται) in verse 19. Now, when Paul says the Gentile believers are fellow-citizens with the saints, these saints, according to the context, are clearly Jewish saints. So, when Paul says the Ephesian Gentiles are "fellow"-citizens, he assumes they are citizens of the same commonwealth as those Jewish saints. In other words, they are citizens of Israel. Thus, Paul directly asserts here that Gentile believers are citizens of the commonwealth of Israel and no longer foreigners. In fact, he uses two additional words that solidly affirm this new reality in a most explicit way. He says the Gentile believers are no longer "strangers and aliens." The words "strangers and aliens" refer to the status of Gentiles who lived in the land, but who were not permitted to enter the congregation (QAHAL) or commonwealth of Israel. The term "stranger" often meant someone outside the congregation of Israel (Ruth 2:10; Lamentations 5:2; Ephesians 2:12). The word "alien" was also frequently used in a similar fashion (Exodus 12:45; Leviticus 22:10; 25:6, 45, 47; Numbers 35:15; Deuteronomy 14:21; 2 Samuel 1:13). Gentile believers are pictured here, then, as entering the commonwealth or congregation (QAHAL) of Israel. They no longer occupy the status of the foreigners and aliens who are excluded from God's assembly and nation.

In summary, it seems to me that these are powerful and cogent reasons to claim that there is explicit evidence for the membership of physically uncircumcised Gentile believers in the New Israel of God of Ephesians 2:11-19. It is not, however, as if Dispensational interpreters are without their own opinion with regard to the teaching of this passage. I have not seen the precise arguments I have brought forward addressed, but I have seen comments on Ephesians 2:11-19 that manifest awareness of the difficulties it poses for the Dispensational distinction between Israel and the Church. Once more I turn to Vlach in order to avoid misrepresenting the "anti-supersessionists":

> Ephesians 2:11–22 shows that Gentiles who used to be far from God have now been brought near God because of Christ. Thus, the soteriological status of believing Gentiles has changed. They now share with Israel in Israel's covenants and promises but they do not become Israel.

> Believing Gentiles cannot be incorporated into Israel because Paul says they are now part of a new structure–the new man.

> Howard Taylor: "Superficial logic has continued to argue that there is no more uniqueness for the Jew and physical Israel. Since it is said Christ has broken down the barrier between Jew and Gentile [Eph. 2:11–18], Israel's election is finished. But this is not the logic of the New Testament. Although there is only one way of salvation for both Jew and Gentile, the New Testament teaches

that the Jewish people do still have a unique place in the *historical* working out of God's redemption of the world in Christ.[1]

Let me walk through these paragraphs one at a time. In the first paragraph, Vlach admits this passage teaches a change of soteriological status for believing Gentiles. They now share with Israel in Israel's covenants and promises. He denies, however, that they actually become Israel. Our study of the passage has shown, however, that this interpretation does not do justice to the contents of the passage. In the first place, the passage not only teaches that Gentiles share in the covenants of Israel, but they also share in the commonwealth of Israel. This is the direct assertion of both verses 12-13 and verse 19. Similarly, such membership in Israel is the immediate suggestion of verse 11, where it is implied that believing Gentiles count as the *true* circumcision (cf. Philippians 3:3; Romans 2:25-29). In other words, it directly implies that believing Gentiles become Israelites. In the second place, the passage does not allow the kind of distinction that Modified Dispensationalism asserts with regard to the Church sharing in the blessings of Israel without participating in Israel itself. As we have seen, within the Church there is no distinction between Jews and Gentiles. In fact, such a distinction is impossible. Rather, there is complete *oneness* between the two because of the character of Christ's redeeming work.

But, this brings us to the second paragraph. Vlach argues here that the Church cannot be Old Israel, because the Church is a new man. This statement, however, misses the mark. Amillennialists are not arguing that believing Gentiles become part of the Old Israel. We are affirming that believing Gentiles become part of a *New* Israel. There is no logical contradiction, however, between the Church being a New Israel and a New Man. In fact, this is exactly what the passage teaches. There is a New Israel (reformed and expanded) composed of new men. The New Man is a spiritual Israelite. The New Man is the one incorporated into the (new,

---

[1] Michael Vlach, "12 Reasons Why Supersessionism/Replacement Theology Is Not a Biblical Doctrine," The article may be accessed at http://www.theologicalstudies.citymax.com/page/page/4425336.htm. I accessed it May 25, 2007. The quote from Howard Taylor is footnoted as follows by Vlach: Howard Taylor, "The Continuity of the People of God in Old and New Testaments," *Scottish Bulletin of Evangelical Theology* 3 (1985): 14–15. Emphasis in original.

reformed, and expanded) commonwealth of Israel by the redeeming work of the one who is the embodiment of the New Israel, Jesus Christ Himself.

Finally, Vlach, quoting Taylor, argues in the third paragraph that the Church cannot be Israel because a special place remains for Israel in the unfolding of redemptive history. In my previous comments I, too, have granted this is the case. It is certainly true that the gospel is to the Jew first and also to the Greek (as Paul says in Romans). It is certainly true that ethnic Israel has a place in the purpose of God. Romans 11 predicts that in every generation God is committed to saving a remnant of believing Jews. Old Israel–ethnic Israel–has a strategic place in the purposes of God. This does not mean, however, that the Church is not the New Israel of God composed both of the remnant of believing Jews *and* the believing Gentiles who are grafted in to the one olive tree of God's covenant promises and people.

In conclusion, there is a distinct place for ethnic Israelites *prior* to salvation. But, there is no distinct place for them afterwards. The categories of true circumcision, true Jews and the Israel of God– post-conversion–include *every* believer in Christ. There is indeed a missing element in Vlach's three paragraphs that must not be overlooked. No corollary response is made toward the solid exegesis I have given of this passage. No account is given for the fact that the passage affirms at several different points, and explicitly, that the believing Gentiles are now part of the Israel of God–the commonwealth of Israel.

Chapter 11
From the Doctrinal to the Hermeneutical

Up to this point, I have had the audacity to claim that the Church is presented in the New Testament as the Israel of God not just two times, but many times. MacArthur sets forth a complete misunderstanding and misrepresentation of our position when he asserts that only two passages support the idea of the Church being the Israel of God. Galatians 6:16 and Romans 9:6 do in fact teach this, but several other passages where the term Israel is used teach this as well. Granted, the majority of the uses of Israel in the New Testament are ethnic in character. Nonetheless, there are a number of uses that clearly describe the Church as God's New Israel. Furthermore, synonyms of Israel like circumcision, Jew, seed of Abraham, sons of Abraham, and children of promise are all used with reference to the Church of Christ. Let me also add that the evidence I have cited here is "only the beginning of sorrows" for the Dispensational denial that the Church is Israel after the Spirit. In my book, *The End Times Made Simple*, I cited much more evidence for the truth that the Church is the Israel of God.

But, in my audacity I must be *even viler*. For, I must now affirm and defend the idea (incredible as it may be to Dispensationalists) that concluding that the Church is the Israel of God need not imply a "spiritualizing" or "allegorizing" hermeneutic. In fact, I believe I can say God *literally* fulfills all His promises to ethnic Israel and the addition of the converted Gentiles to God's Israel also *literally* fulfills the Old Testament. Let me repeat once more what I have said previously. The difference between MacArthur and Amillennialism is not whether God keeps His promises to ethnic Israel. It is certainly not whether God's promises to ethnic Israel are finally conditioned on an unaided human response to them.

This is not to say that there are no important hermeneutical differences between MacArthur and us. Yet, however important they are, these differences are not of the kind that MacArthur and his allies imagine. In the next chapter, therefore, let us hermeneutically "boldly go where no man (or at least no Dispensationalist) has gone before."

CHAPTER TWELVE
Who's a Spiritualizer?

As I refreshed my memory of what MacArthur had to say about biblical interpretation in his manifesto, I began to copy and paste the parts of the message with direct bearing on this subject. I discovered around one third of his message was composed of specific comments regarding hermeneutics. Clearly, MacArthur thinks something important is going on in this area. Of course, historically speaking, Dispensational Premillennialism has always emphasized interpretive theory as one of the grand differences between itself and Covenant Theology. To be specific, Dispensationalism claimed it held to a literal interpretation of the Bible, while Amillennialists were spiritualizers.

Three times in his message MacArthur mentions and condemns a spiritualizing method of interpretation. Many more times, though the actual word is not mentioned, the condemnation of spiritualizing is implied. Specifically, MacArthur charges "spiritualizers" with marring the perspicuity or clarity of Scripture. With this method of interpretation, he believes, the text of Scripture may mean anything the interpreter pleases. It is his opinion that this method of interpretation practically represents an end to biblical authority. Here is what he says:

> Is in fact working hard to understand prophetic passages needless, even impossible, because they require a *spiritualized* or allegorized set of interpretations that says the truth is somehow hidden behind the normal meaning of the words so any idea of what it might mean is as good as any other idea of what it might mean since it doesn't mean what it says?

> But the idea that the New Testament is the starting point for understanding the Old Testament is exactly where Amillennialism comes from, reading it back into the Old Testament; and, of course, you damage the perspicuity or the clarity of the sensibility of the Old Testament in and of itself. Such an approach leads to an even more grand kind of *spiritualizing* that goes beyond just prophetic texts and gives license to *spiritualize* other things and to read New Testament Christian principles back into those texts in the Old Testament where they do not rise from a legitimate interpretation.[1]

These are serious charges. I would be really worried if I thought they applied to me or my understanding of hermeneutics. I would be terrified if I was one who believed in spiritualizing. I think those who do hold such an allegorical or spiritualizing hermeneutic–and there are people who do–should repent and bring forth exegesis fitting for repentance. It is really wrong to put textual scarves into the black-top hat of interpretation and magically produce hermeneutical bunnies. I think there are some people who have held something akin to my eschatology who have naively or dangerously done this. Let me simply say that I believe they are wrong and in some cases terribly misguided.[2]

But as for me and my house, we will serve the Lord and not adopt or defend spiritualizing. Because this is my stance, and I believe the view of most Reformed interpreters today, it has always seemed to me that the supposed hermeneutical chasm between Dispensationalism and Covenant Theology has never been as wide or deep as suggested. Of course, I am not saying that there are no differences whatsoever. It only seems to me that the differences between us are rather quantitative than qualitative.

---

[1] The emphasis on the three occurrences of *spiritualize* is mine.

[2] The premier example of spiritualizing in an Amillennialist may be Harold Kamping, whose book *1994?* (New York: Vantage Press, 1992) and sermons are filled with the worst kind of spiritualizing, hyper-typology, and allegorizing. Of course, Harold Kamping scarcely represents a Reformed and Covenantal approach to the Scriptures. I have seen other examples among Amillennialists or anti-Dispensationalists of what I think is a naïve, spiritualizing hermeneutic. I also think that those Amillennialists who have found the fulfillment of the kingdom only in the gospel age and not also in the consummate Church in the new and redeemed earth have engaged in a kind of spiritualizing.

This last assertion will probably fill MacArthur and our other Dispensational friends with amazement. They will wonder, of course, *how in the world* I can say this. They assume that anyone who believes the Church is the Israel of God must spiritualize and allegorize Scripture. Certainly, they have a right to their opinion. Yet, I hope to show a way of interpreting the Bible not qualitatively different than their own (which does not indulge allegorizing or spiritualizing), which actually affirms the Church is the Israel of God.

CHAPTER THIRTEEN
Literal, Normal, Factual, Face-Value, Specific Interpretation

There is an important lesson to be learned from the following statements in MacArthur's message. Take a look at them and see if you can discover the identity of this lesson:

> ...the truth is somehow hidden behind the *normal meaning* of the words so any idea of what it might mean is as good as any other idea of what it might mean since it doesn't mean what it says...

> ...there is nothing in the text that gives any kind of mandate to indicate that this is something other than *specific, literal, normal, factual language*....

> ...all eschatology will unfold with magnificent beauty. With the *normal hermeneutic* [applied consistently],...

> I would be absolutely lost in the Old Testament if I couldn't take the Scripture at its *face value*.

> If you affirm a *normal hermeneutic*....

What is the lesson to be learned from such statements? Simply that it is not so easy to define what literal interpretation is. MacArthur needs many other descriptive words to tell us what he means by a literal interpretation. He means *specific, normal, factual,* and *face-value* interpretation. My point is that the term, literal, is not self-identifying or self-interpreting. MacArthur has to labor to tell us what he means.

MacArthur's struggles are reflective of the enormous debates today among evangelical scholars over the meaning of "literal" interpretation. I do not have time nor do I need to trace out those debates. But, suffice it to say that the definition of literal interpretation cannot be taken for granted today. For instance, I was raised on the idea that we should interpret the Bible literally. But even the staunch Dispensationalists who were my spiritual teachers when I was young could not simply say this in an unqualified way, because they knew that there were passages in the Bible that could not be taken literally. The fall-back position then became that we must interpret the Bible literally *wherever possible*. Today, this qualification of literal interpretation also seems hopelessly naïve to me. Take, for example, Revelation 13:1:

> And the dragon stood on the sand of the seashore. Then I saw a beast coming up out of the sea, having ten horns and seven heads, and on his horns *were* ten diadems, and on his heads *were* blasphemous names.

I believe the Dispensationalist teachers who taught me the "literal wherever possible" view would have, without exception, understood this text symbolically. I suppose they might have argued that the assertion of Revelation 13:1 is not literally possible. But today I have the sense (and perhaps the audacity) to ask, Why not? What is so impossible about understanding this verse with strict literality? Is it impossible for God to create dragons and beasts with ten horns and seven heads? I think it is possible. Thus, the "literal wherever possible" hermeneutic does not satisfy the needs of this text or properly qualify literal interpretation. This is why MacArthur wants to speak of a *normal* hermeneutic. He needs to qualify the meaning of "literal interpretation" to explain texts like Revelation 13:1.

Given this view of hermeneutics, we are able to see why MacArthur can easily cite Covenant theologians as rejecting literal interpretation. MacArthur quotes, for instance, three Covenant theologians who argue that the Old Testament prophecies cannot be taken "literally."

> O.T. Allis, a well-known Amillennialist, writing in *Prophecy and the Church*, says, "The Old Testament prophecies, if literally interpreted, cannot be regarded as having been yet fulfilled or

being capable of fulfillment in the present age." That was a problem for him.

Floyd Hamilton in *The Basis of the Millennial Faith* said, "Now we must frankly admit that a literal interpretation of the Old Testament prophecies gives us just such a picture of an earthly reign of the Messiah as the Premillennialist pictures."

Another Amillennialist, Loraine Boettner in *The Meaning of the Millennium*, said, "It is generally agreed that if the prophecies are taken literally, that they do foretell a restoration of the nation of Israel in the land of Palestine with the Jews having a prominent place in that kingdom and ruling over the other nations."

Such statements as these, however, should not be viewed as proof that these men have departed into spiritualizing. The dichotomy between literal and spiritualizing interpretation is of MacArthur's and Dispensationalism's own making. The problem is the term literal, as we have noted, has a variety of connotations. Boettner, Allis, and Hamilton are simply affirming that the Bible contains symbolic language which must be interpreted symbolically. I do not think they reject most of what MacArthur means to affirm when he promotes literal interpretation. They would not deny that most of the Bible should be interpreted in a more literal fashion. In the quotations MacArthur gives they are not using literal as over against spiritual. Rather, they are using literal as opposed to symbolic. I do not believe for a moment that MacArthur would deny the presence of symbols in the Bible which should be interpreted symbolically. MacArthur's normal, face-value hermeneutic encompasses both symbolic and poetic language. This is why, I think, he qualifies literal interpretation with so many synonyms.

Of course, it is not as though there is no confusion at this point in the way MacArthur and his supporters write or speak. I found this interesting statement on Vlach's website. It illustrates the confusion to which I am pointing.

Approach prophetic/apocalyptic literature with the same historical-grammatical-literary approach that you would use when interpreting other portions of Scripture. Coming into contact with prophetic literature does not mean that we switch our hermeneutical approach. Realize that behind each symbol and figure of speech in prophetic literature is a literal truth. *The presence of symbols does not mean that symbolical or allegorical interpretation is necessary.*[1]

I find this truly confusing.

It is, however, the same kind of confusion I spy in MacArthur's manifesto. Notice how Vlach, like MacArthur, makes the point that we should not switch our hermeneutical approach when we come to prophecy. Vlach says, "Coming into contact with prophetic literature does not mean that we switch our hermeneutical approach." Similarly, MacArthur argues:

> In all three cases, that proved to them to be a serious problem and required a severe alteration in hermeneutics at each of those prophetic passages in order to avoid a Premillennial conclusion, a fate worse than death. [Laughter from audience]

> So, to protect some kind of preconception it is necessary to change the rules of interpretation. Now if we're going to change those rules, I think we need a word from God. We better have a word from God because He cares that we get it right.

> I don't think God wants us to change the rules of interpretation when we go to Genesis 1 to 3.

What does this mean? On the one hand, no one (at least I know of no one) advocates a wholly different hermeneutic for interpreting prophetic passages. On the other hand, isn't it obvious that we have to interpret different kinds of literature differently? Apparently this is not so obvious to Vlach and MacArthur. While to me it seems clear that Vlach and MacArthur are admitting the reality of different kinds of literature, they also seem to say this reality should make no difference in the way we interpret such passages. Can they really mean this? Do they really mean to say that we must interpret symbolic and apocalyptic language literally? Apparently they do mean this. Again, here are Vlach's words, "The presence of symbols

---

[1] Michael Vlach, "Interpreting Biblical Prophecy." The article may be accessed at http://www.theologicalstudies.citymax.com/page/page/4425336.htm. I accessed it July 15, 2007. The emphasis is mine.

does not mean that symbolical or allegorical interpretation is necessary."

Well, *please*, one would have thought the presence of symbols would have *exactly* meant that some symbolical interpretation is necessary. Of course, the presence of symbols does not mean that *allegorical* interpretation is necessary. But, this is precisely the problem. Vlach seems to equate symbolical interpretation with allegorical interpretation. I do not. Symbols should not be interpreted allegorically. They should be interpreted–well–*symbolically*.

Here's the point. Any comprehensive hermeneutic must take into account the fact that there are different literary genres in the Bible. We agree that all interpretation should be historical and grammatical. I have a feeling this is sometimes what MacArthur mainly means by literal interpretation. I do not agree, however, that the assertion of historical-grammatical interpretation provides a complete hermeneutic. We must also affirm the necessity of literary genre interpretation. This is to say, interpretation must take into account the literary genre of the passage in question.[2] Not all prophetic literature is symbolic, but some of it–especially in Daniel and Revelation–is certainly symbolic or (as the biblical scholars say) apocalyptic. Because such passages are apocalyptic, they must be interpreted figuratively and symbolically in accordance with the apocalyptic genre or form. Daniel 7:2-8 provides an example of such literature:

---

[2] It is also relevant to note that a comprehensive hermeneutic must take into account the necessity of a theological interpretation of the Bible. The Bible has both a divine and human authorship. Historical-grammatical interpretation goes no further than the human authorship. It asks only what the original human author might or could have meant by what he wrote. The Bible affirms for itself in addition divine authorship. Granted, what the divine author meant in any given passage will not contradict what the human authors meant. Yet, it must be obvious that the intention of the divine author could go considerably beyond what the human author meant or could have meant. This is the fundamental defect in the hermeneutical views of Walt Kaiser whom MacArthur quotes. Here is MacArthur's quotation of Kaiser: "If you say that the Old Testament cannot be rightly interpreted apart from the New Testament, then you have denied the perspicuity of the Old Testament, and as Walt Kaiser puts it, 'Now you have a canon within a canon.'"

[2] Daniel said, "I was looking in my vision by night, and behold, the four winds of heaven were stirring up the great sea. [3] "And four great beasts were coming up from the sea, different from one another. [4] "The first *was* like a lion and had *the* wings of an eagle. I kept looking until its wings were plucked, and it was lifted up from the ground and made to stand on two feet like a man; a human mind also was given to it. [5] "And behold, another beast, a second one, resembling a bear. And it was raised up on one side, and three ribs *were* in its mouth between its teeth; and thus they said to it, 'Arise, devour much meat!' [6] "After this I kept looking, and behold, another one, like a leopard, which had on its back four wings of a bird; the beast also had four heads, and dominion was given to it. [7] "After this I kept looking in the night visions, and behold, a fourth beast, dreadful and terrifying and extremely strong; and it had large iron teeth. It devoured and crushed, and trampled down the remainder with its feet; and it was different from all the beasts that were before it, and it had ten horns. [8] "While I was contemplating the horns, behold, another horn, a little one, came up among them, and three of the first horns were pulled out by the roots before it; and behold, this horn possessed eyes like the eyes of a man, and a mouth uttering great *boasts*.

Later, Daniel 7:16 proves the language above must be symbolically interpreted. "I approached one of those who were standing by and began asking him the exact meaning of all this. So he told me and made known to me the interpretation of these things..." The prophet does not respond to the vision by saying, "No problem. I see exactly what these words mean. It's simple, if I merely apply the principles of literal interpretation." No, Daniel 7:16 makes clear that the visions seen by the inner eye of the prophet (or apostle) do not entail *normal language* that can be taken at *face-value*. They require interpretation precisely because they are figurative. Unlike literal language or prose, their meaning is not immediately obvious to us.

The interpretation of Daniel and Revelation must, therefore, take into account the apocalyptic-symbolic character of the literature. This does not mean we adopt a wholly new hermeneutic. It only means we utilize the hermeneutic we always employ. This hermeneutic is historical-grammatical interpretation which takes into account the literary genre of the passage in question. In other words, we must interpret passages containing symbols historically, grammatically, *and* symbolically. Only such interpretation is in accord with their literary genre. I think MacArthur and Vlach actually know this. Yet, they somehow do not take it into account when they describe their hermeneutic and desire, instead, to assert they interpret the Bible literally.

CHAPTER FOURTEEN
The Case of Genesis 1-3

That a kind of symbolical interpretation is necessary becomes clear in MacArthur in spite of himself. This is seen in his comments on Genesis 1-3. It is common for Dispensationalists to accuse Amillennialists of occupying a hermeneutical slippery-slope that leads to Liberalism and, specifically, a less than literal interpretation of the creation days. In turn, they imply, this paves the way for evolutionary views of the origin of the world and the human race. MacArthur generally follows this tactic. Here is what he says:

> I don't think God wants us to change the rules of interpretation when we go to Genesis 1-3. I don't think God is pleased when we come up with progressive creationism, theistic evolution or any kind of day-age view of Genesis 1-3. Rather, God is exalted as the Creator in the full glory of His creative power when we take Genesis 1-3 at face-value. There is no other way to take it because there is nothing in the text that gives any kind of mandate to indicate that this is something other than specific, literal, normal, factual language. Really you can't even justify calling it poetry because that doesn't work. Recent studies conducted by one of our professors at The Masters College, reducing the Creation account linguistically to a computer program and graphing the comparison between prose and poetry, led to the very interesting conclusion-- that there is 99.9% evidence that this is prose and no possibility that it is poetry. We don't want anybody tampering with the beginning. Why are we so tolerant of people tampering with the end? And why, when we don't want to arbitrarily allow somebody to introduce their own hermeneutics to Genesis 1-3, are we content to allow people to introduce their own hermeneutics into prophetic passages throughout the Bible and particularly in the Book of Revelation? Where is the divine mandate on the pages of the Bible

to do this? What passage is it in? What verse? Where is it? And who decides then the new rules for engagement?

I happen to be a six literal day creationist. I also happen to think that studies like the one MacArthur mentions are fairly compelling evidence for a prosaic rather than poetic interpretation of Genesis 1-3.[1] But there are hermeneutical implications in what he says that MacArthur wants us conveniently to overlook.

In the first place, why did this professor even need to do such a study? Doesn't The Masters College hold a literal hermeneutic? Doesn't MacArthur think that the whole Bible is to be taken literally without exception and everywhere? Why, then, go to the expense and bother to show that Genesis 1-3 is more like historical narrative (literal language) than poetry?

But that brings me to the second thing hidden in MacArthur's argument here. Where did the poetic passages with which Genesis 1-3 was compared come from? *They came from the Bible.* If you read the study, the other Hebrew poetic passages to which Genesis 1-3 was compared came from the Hebrew Old Testament.[2] Only such passages from the Old Testament provide a true comparison. This is why MacArthur thinks such a study is significant. He knows that in the Bible there are poetic, symbolic, parabolic, and apocalyptic passages that should and must be interpreted poetically, symbolically, parabolically, and apocalyptically–not as prosaic language or historical narrative. MacArthur believes, I think, that interpreting such passages in such ways is consistent with a literal interpretation of the Bible. I will grant him his definition of literal interpretation.

Yet having said this, I must qualify my allowance of his definition of literal interpretation. The reason is that one could easily imagine someone properly saying, "The parable of the four soils must be interpreted symbolically–not literally." MacArthur in other places contrasts literal interpretation with symbolic interpretation. Thus, he has to clarify or be more forthright about the fact that some

---

[1] MacArthur is referring to the study published by Stephen W. Boyd, "The Biblical Hebrew Creation Account: New Numbers Tell the Story," *Impact* # 377 (November, 2004), i-iv. Boyd is described there as Associate Professor of Bible at The Master's College in Santa Clarita, California.

[2] Boyd, "The Biblical Hebrew Creation Account: New Numbers Tell the Story," *Impact* # 377 (November, 2004), i-iv.

interpretation of symbols as symbols is consistent with his definition of literal interpretation. Second, he must understand that *in principle* he has granted by such a definition of literal interpretation all that Covenant theologians are affirming in their understanding of a biblical hermeneutic that takes into account the literary genre of a given passage.

With regard to Genesis 1-3, let me say that MacArthur's slippery-slope argument against Amillennialists is undone by his implicit admission that there are other passages in the Bible that ought not to be interpreted as historical narrative or, in other words, *literally*. MacArthur, by citing this study, virtually admits that there are poetic passages in the Hebrew Old Testament that ought to be interpreted poetically not *literally*. This being the case, it is not somehow heretical merely to raise the question of the literary genre of Genesis 1-3. Neither is it on the slippery-slope to heresy to argue that the literary genre of large portions of Daniel and Revelation (and other prophetic passages) is clearly apocalyptic and that this means that they must be interpreted not only historically and grammatically, but also symbolically.

Another matter comes up for discussion here. MacArthur repeatedly argues (as he does at the beginning of the above quotation) that Amillennialists are changing the rules of interpretation for the sake of their eschatology.

> In all three cases, that proved to them to be a serious problem and required a severe alteration in hermeneutics at each of those prophetic passages in order to avoid a Premillennial conclusion, a fate worse than death. [Laughter from audience]

> So, to protect some kind of preconception it is necessary to change the rules of interpretation. Now if we're going to change those rules, I think we need a word from God. We better have a word from God because He cares that we get it right.

This is a serious charge. It is one, however, that has some application to MacArthur himself. If he finds the argument of The Master's College professor helpful, it must be because he himself recognizes that the rules do in some sense change depending on whether one is interpreting a prosaic passage or a poetic passage. Otherwise his enthusiastic endorsement of the study makes no sense.

The Bible must always be interpreted according to its literary genre. I would argue that interpreting the Bible according to its literary genre is not necessarily contrary to literal interpretation. That is to say, a literal kind of hermeneutic does not need to deny that there are different literary genres in the Bible, some more or less prosaic or literal and others more or less symbolic or poetic. Define literal interpretation as simply taking these passages as they are intended by God. Define literal interpretation simply as historical-grammatical interpretation. If this is the way you define literal interpretation, then taking into account the literary genre of the passage supplements and is consistent with literal interpretation and does not contradict it. Whatever God intends to say through the different literary genres contained in the Bible we take as the literal truth. We do not search for a hidden meaning behind the literal truth conveyed through the historical narrative or poetic song or apocalyptic vision.

I also need to respond to MacArthur's often repeated concern that non-literal interpretation (what he calls spiritualizing) leads to terrible confusion as to the meaning of Scripture so that there is an end to any practical ability to preach the Bible with authority. This concern is legitimate, if you mean by spiritualizing something like Harold Kamping practices in his preaching and writing. But let me make clear that taking into account the literary genre and symbolic character of a passage do not lead to terrible confusion about the meaning of Scripture or the erosion of scriptural authority. Let me address both literary genre and symbolism.

Let me say something about deciding the literary genre of a passage. It is clearly wrong to allow any consideration external to Scripture itself (like the reigning scientific paradigms) to dictate how we interpret Scripture. This is what many have allowed to happen in their interpretation of Genesis 1-3. Scripture itself is and must be determinative of its own literary genre. Two things are important here, but both derive from the fundamental principle of allowing Scripture to interpret Scripture.

First, as MacArthur himself clearly implies by citing the study of the literary genre of Genesis 1-3, there are internal signs in the passage itself, including its grammar, which distinguish its literary genre and mark it as prosaic or historical narrative. The markers which the study in question cites constitute one form such internal signs may take.

Second, if the interpretation of a given passage as literal, in the sense of being prosaic or historical narrative, seems to conflict with the plain teaching of other Scripture, this may be an important indication that it is not intended as literal in the sense of being prosaic or historical narrative. I would and do argue that the prophecy of sin offerings being offered by Levitical priests in Ezekiel (40:39; 42:13; 43:19, 21, 22, 25; 44:27, 29; 45:17, 19, 22, 23, 25; 46:20)–if taken as predicting something yet future form our vantage point–is a plain contradiction of the teaching of Ephesians 2 and the Book of Hebrews. This is an important indication that this entire passage in its literary genre is not "literal." These two indications enable the interpreter to avoid subjectivity in his understanding of the literary genre of any given passage.

Let me also say something about the interpretation of biblical symbols. The mere recognition by both MacArthur and Vlach of the fact that there are symbols in the Bible shows that there is no necessary connection between the presence of symbols and wild subjectivity in our interpretation of the Bible. Again, the key is that Scripture must be used to interpret Scripture. First, biblical symbols are often interpreted in the context of their usage itself. This is the case, for instance, several times in the parables of the Lord found in Matthew 13. Second, biblical symbols often may be illumined by parallels found in the context. Here, for instance, we think of the twin parables of the mustard seed and the leaven. Third, biblical symbols are also borrowed from historically previous parts of the canon where their meaning is made clear. Again, the point I am making is that "symbolical interpretation" is not to be feared as if it were the inevitable path to confusion in biblical interpretation. If MacArthur and Vlach admit the presence of symbols in the Bible, and if they still think clear biblical interpretation is possible, then they themselves at some level admit this conclusion to be true.

Excursus on the Genre and
Interpretation of Revelation 20:1-10

One of my correspondents challenged the hermeneutical method I expound in this chapter by saying, "Let us go right to the heart of it...In the context of Revelation 20, what gives you or anyone else the indication that 1000 is a symbolic number? I ask the question to point out the subjective nature you impose upon the text."[3]

Below is my response to the important question this correspondent poses. It differs only slightly from what I posted on our blog.[4]

The 1000 years of Revelation 20–are they literal? The literary genre of the passage is crucial. There is no reason to exempt the numbers of any passage from the literary genre of the passage. No. If the genre of the passage is figurative, then the assumption must be that the numbers are figurative. So here we have the imprisonment of the devil for 1,000 years. The idea of a prison is crucial to verses 1-3 and verses 7-10. Is the inmate of the prison a literal dragon or serpent? No, in this case the passage actually identifies the symbol as referring to the devil. Is the key of the prison literal? No, of course not. Satan is a spiritual being. What good would a literal key do? Is the chain of the prison a literal chain, like that used on Paul in Acts 16 (a narrative passage, by the way)? No, of course not. What good would a physical or literal chain do on a spiritual being? He'd fade right through it like Voldemort in Harry Potter. Is the prison, called the "abyss," literal or physical? Well, I would agree that it is some place, but beyond that I do not think we should conclude there is a literal hole in the ground. It also is not literal. So let's get this straight. The inmate, the key, the chain, and even the prison itself are symbolic representations of different aspects of God's binding of Satan, but the prison sentence–the 1,000 years–must be taken literally? This sounds very inconsistent to me–not to say arbitrary.

In Revelation 20 Premillennialists argue that there is affirmed a future, interim binding of Satan. Can one cite even one parallel passage for such a doctrine? Amillennialists can cite many parallel passages for the idea that as a result of the work of Christ Satan has been restrained in the present age (Matthew 12:24-29; Luke 10:17-19; John 12:31-32; Colossians 2:15; Hebrews 2:14; 1 John 3:8; Revelation 12:5-10). Only the interpretation that sees Satan bound in Christ's first advent is supported by the analogy of faith. A future,

---

[3] I am well aware that what follows is not a thorough treatment or interpretation of Revelations 20:1-10. For this see my book, *The End Times Made Simple* (Amityville, NY: Calvary Press, 2003).

[4] http://www.mctsowensboro.org/blog/.

provisional binding of Satan is unknown elsewhere in Scripture and is, therefore, purely speculative and conjectural. Its sole exegetical basis is the Premillennial interpretation of Revelation 20. The choice here is between interpreting symbols symbolically and biblically or interpreting them in a woodenly literal way that refuses to take into account the literary genre of the passage. I think the option we should choose is obvious.

In reply to a further response from this correspondent I made a number of replies. I excerpt three of them which I think are crucial to the present discussion. I think the reader can discern the nature of this further response from my replies to it.

First, you think that angels are physical as well as spiritual beings and, I suppose, you must think this to sustain your hermeneutic.

Second, you change the subject to the earthly kingdom idea when I point out that there is no parallel passage which points to a future, provisional binding of Satan. I stand by my assertion. The point is that your interpretation is contrary to the analogy of faith. The point is not that God has to say things more than once for us to believe them. The question is whether He has actually said them even once.

Third, again and again you assume that I disagree with you when you say that symbolic language points to something real. "Real" is my word. You use the words "actual" and "literal" and "physical," but this leads to the idea that angels have physical bodies which I dispute. Anyway, I think what you mean by literal is real and not necessarily physical. I do agree that the symbols of the Scripture point to something real and actual. I do not agree that they necessarily point to something physical. There are real and actual things that are not physical in the normal sense like our souls and spirits and especially like God. God is a rock means that He is strong and faithful. The divine attributes of strength and faithfulness are not essentially physical. They are real and have, of course, physical applications.

Here is the bottom-line. Of course, the symbols of Scripture point to something real and often it is even physical, but they do so symbolically and must be interpreted symbolically in order to attain to the literal truth they convey. This is one of the key problems in this argument. Literal can mean real and it can mean physical. I accept literal interpretation in the sense that I believe in realism in scriptural interpretation. I do not accept literal interpretation, if it means that we do not recognize in the Scriptures literary genres that are more or less figurative (or if it means that we have to deny that biblical symbols must be interpreted symbolically).

CHAPTER FIFTEEN
How Can "Literal" Interpretation Conclude the Church is Israel?

At this point, I feel a need to recap the argument. Let me do so by reminding us all that MacArthur claims that Amillennialists believe in supersessionism or replacement theology. This is the beginning of his chain of reasoning. He concludes that, believing in replacement theology wherein the Church simply replaces Israel in the plan of God, we must and do believe in a spiritualizing or allegorizing hermeneutic.

Here is my counter-argument. First, I have asserted that Amillennialists today do not (or at least do not have to) believe in replacement theology. Or in other words, they do not need to assert and in most cases do not assert that the Church simply replaces Israel. I recently discovered that my view of this matter is corroborated by O. Palmer Robertson in his wonderful book *The Israel of God*. I highly commend this book to all who read this and especially to my Dispensational brethren. Let me give you a couple of choice statements that he makes:

> From this point on, it is not that the church takes the place of Israel, but that a renewed Israel of God is being formed by the shaping of the Church. This kingdom will reach beyond the limits of the Israel of the old covenant. Although Jesus begins with the Israel of old, he will not allow his kingdom to be limited by its borders.[1]

> The domain of this kingdom, the realm of Messiah's rule, would indeed begin at Jerusalem, the focal point of Israel's life for

---

[1] Robertson, *The Israel of God*, 118.

centuries. So unquestionably, Israel would be a primary participant in the coming of the messianic kingdom. Jesus was not teaching a "replacement" theology in which all connection with the promises given to the fathers is summarily settled, and the Israel of old is replaced by the church of the present day. [2]

These quotations lead into and imply the second point of my counter-argument. It is the one I come to in this section of these studies. Since we do not believe in supersessionism or replacement theology, we do not hold or need to hold a spiritualizing or allegorical hermeneutic. There is a way within the bounds of historical-grammatical interpretation supplemented by a recognition of, first, the divine authorship of Scripture (theological interpretation) and, second, the diverse literary genres of Scripture (literary-genre interpretation) to say that the Church is the Israel of God. It is not necessary to fall into some sort of lunatic, fringe spiritualizing to come to this conclusion.

Let me put this in different terms. I think that the hermeneutic I described deserves the label "literal interpretation." Let me call it a "realistic literal interpretation." Historical-grammatical-theological-literary genre interpretation provides a kind of "realistic-literal method of interpretation." It does not assert that the symbols of Scripture point to "airy nothings." It agrees with the MacArthurs of the world that they point to "real somethings." It is realist and, in this sense, literal. But it holds that the Bible sometimes speaks of these "real somethings" by using symbolic language. Thus, this interpretation differs from what I will call "woodenly literal interpretation" which refuses to recognize either the fact or hermeneutical significance of the symbolic literary genres of Scripture.

Within the bounds of this "literal" method of interpretation, let me now show the path by which the Scriptures come to assert that the Church is the Israel of God (Galatians 6:16).

---

[2] Robertson, *The Israel of God*, 133.

CHAPTER SIXTEEN
The Literal Truth about
the Church Being Israel

A great deal might be said about the redemptive-historical justification and hermeneutical reasons why the Scriptures may assert that the Church is God's Israel. I will only give here a synopsis of the relevant material. Again, I want to recommend O. Palmer Robertson's *The Israel of God*.

The very first thing I want to say is that the Church has an ethnically Jewish origin and constitution. Once I heard a radio preacher arguing that everything up to Acts 10 in the New Testament was Jewish ground. I did not disagree, because I think that everything afterwards is Jewish ground as well. The whole New Testament (let's be clear about it) is Jewish ground. Why do I affirm that the Church is a Jewish institution?

I affirm this, first of all, because Jesus the Christ was and had to be an ethnic Jew (Matthew 1:1-18). Jesus Christ is, however, in His office as Messiah and Mediator the origin and center of the Church's existence. When he said that he would build His Church, He had just been named "the Christ, the Son of the living God" by Peter (Matthew 16:16-19). So it was as Messiah of the Jews that He would build His Church. The Church is, then, the Church of the Messiah. It is no longer merely the "Church of Israel" (QAHAL ISRAEL) or "Church of Yahweh" (QAHAL YAHWEH) mentioned so often in the Old Testament. It is now eschatological Israel, the Church of the Messiah (QAHAL MASHIACH). Thus, Paul argues in Galatians 3 that Christ is the true seed of Abraham and that all who are in union with him (Galatians 3:29) are also Abraham's seed and heirs according to promise (Galatians 3:29).

And speaking of promises, Paul also affirms that all the promises of God to Israel are ratified in Christ and affirms that we as His Church–both Jews and Gentiles–are beneficiaries of those promises. Just as in Galatians 3:29, so also in 2 Corinthians 1:19-20 this is confirmed.

> [19] For the Son of God, Christ Jesus, who was preached among you by us - by me and Silvanus and Timothy - was not yes and no, but is yes in Him. [20] For as many as are the promises of God, in Him they are yes; therefore also through Him is our Amen to the glory of God through us.

So the Church lives on the basis of the promises of God, and these promises belong to her because she is in union with the Christ who is the ethnic seed of Abraham. Thus, the Church also is the seed of Abraham and heir of all the promises made to the seed of Abraham. The Church has a Jewish Savior and Redeemer.

The Church also has a Jewish foundation. The church is built on the foundation of the Apostles (Matthew 16:16-19; Ephesians 2:20; Revelation 21:14). The Apostles of Christ, even including Paul and James the Lord's brother, were all ethnic Jews. The Gentiles who come to Christ and into the Church are built on a Jewish foundation and so become part of a Jewish house.

Yet further, the Church has in every generation a Jewish nucleus. According to Romans 11 God has an elect Jewish remnant in every generation. The Church is the one olive tree of Romans 11:16-24. It has a Jewish root and trunk. Additionally, it has believing Jewish branches and Gentile branches grafted in through the work of the Spirit and by faith. The accumulation of this Jewish remnant from every generation make up the fulfillment of the "all Israel" (a reference to ethnic Israel) who will be saved, just as the fullness of the Gentiles is the sum total of the "elect Gentiles."

For all these reasons, I affirm that the Church is in a physical and ethnic sense a Jewish institution. The Church has an ethnically Jewish Messiah, an ethnically Jewish apostolic foundation, and an ethnically Jewish membership nucleus. According to Ephesians 2:12-19, it is "the commonwealth of Israel" with both ethnically Jewish citizens and now formerly Gentile citizens who have become New Israelites by the circumcision made without hands (Colossians 2:11).

Much more remains to be said. This, however, should at least begin to satisfy anyone who is concerned for the rights of ethnic Jews and a "literal interpretation" of the Bible.[1]

---

[1] This chapter and a number of others raised the question of the meaning of Romans 11 in the minds of correspondents. For my understanding of Romans 11, see Appendix One at the end of the book.

CHAPTER SEVENTEEN
The Church as the Elect Remnant of Israel

It is not as though MacArthur does not know the doctrine of the remnant. At one point at least, he states it quite clearly.

> Through history there has always been an Israel of God, there has always been a remnant, there have always been those who did not bow the knee to Baal. God always has had a people; there have always been His chosen ones. Not all Israel is Israel; that is to say, not all of ethnic Israel is the true Israel of God, true believers. But God has always had a remnant; He has always had a people--as Isaiah 6 says, a "stump," a "holy seed"--throughout history. But in the future there will be a salvation of ethnic Israel on a national level, and that's the message of Jeremiah 31. Here is the New Covenant; it was also given to Israel. We like to talk about the New Covenant because we participate in the salvation provision of the New Covenant ratified in the death of Christ. But the original pledge of the New Covenant is in a special way given to a future generation of Jews.

Even in this quotation, however, MacArthur reveals what the heart of his understanding of the Jewish promises is. He is focused on the fulfillment of the promises by a future, national conversion of ethnic Israel. Thus, even though he knows the doctrine of the remnant, it does not seem to count as a fulfillment of the promises to Israel. Notice the repeated future focus in the following quotations:

> As it does, the perpetuity of the elect Church to salvation glory, so the Scripture in similar language and by promises from the same God affirms the perpetuity of ethnic Israel to a future salvation of a generation of Jews that will fulfill all divine promises given to them by God.

Now that the Spirit of God is moving the Church to reestablish the glorious high ground of sovereign grace in salvation, it is time to reestablish the equally high ground of sovereign grace for a future generation of ethnic Israel in salvation and the Messianic earthly kingdom, with the complete fulfillment of all God's promises to Israel.

I am unwaveringly committed to the sovereign election of a future generation of Jews to salvation and the full inheritance of all the promises and covenants of God given to them in the Old Testament because the truth of God's Word is at stake.

We have to give the world the truth about the end of history and the climactic glory of Christ and the fulfillment of God's promises to Israel and the Church.

If you affirm a normal hermeneutic and the perspicuity of the Old Testament, it pronounces clearly covenants and promises and a kingdom to come to ethnic Israel.

The fact that there are some Jews that don't believe does not nullify the faithfulness of God. Just because there are some whom God chooses, doesn't mean that He's not going to choose a whole, duly-constituted generation of Jews to fulfill His promises [in the future].

At one point MacArthur actually reveals what can only be called an exclusively future focus on the future fulfillment of God's promises. Look at this:

And there are only two people [groups of human beings] elections in Scripture: Israel (an eschatological group of ethnic Israelites that will constitute the future nation who will receive the promises of God) and the Church.

MacArthur here completely discounts the present or past election of a Jewish remnant as in any way counting with regard to the election of Israel or the fulfillment of promises to Israel. That is fulfilled only in "an eschatological group of ethnic Israelites that will constitute the future nation." This election of a future generation of Israelites and the election of the Church are the only two people elections in the Bible.

Because MacArthur so completely discounts the past and present elect remnant from the Jews, he thinks that Amillennialists believe that there is absolutely no fulfillment of the promises to the Jewish nation.

> Sure, Israel sinned, became apostate, killed the Son of God. That's it. Israel's out and forfeits everything. The church gets it all *if* she can do better than Israel. So far doesn't look real hopeful.

> Amillennialism makes no sense because it basically says Israel, on its own, forfeited all the promises. Do you think, on their own, they could've done something to guarantee they'd receive them?

But this argument wholly ignores the fact that Amillennialists argue that throughout history God's promises were fulfilled in an elect remnant of ethnic Jews. Here is my point. If MacArthur does not everywhere discount the doctrine of the Jewish remnant, he yet discounts it sufficiently that he misses both its biblical significance and its significance for Amillennialists.

First of all, the idea (once explicitly asserted by MacArthur, but many times implied) that the only meaningful fulfillment of the promises to Israel takes place in the millennium to a future generation of Jews is wholly unbiblical. It means that nothing that happened in the Old Testament conquest of the land or in Old Testament Israel's long abode in the land counts as fulfillment of God's promises. This is nonsense. The conquest of the land under Joshua counted as fulfillment of God's covenant promises–even though that promise was not fulfilled except to a small remnant of the original people involved in the Exodus from Egypt. Notice the following key statements from Joshua.

> Joshua 1:2 Moses My servant is dead; now therefore arise, cross this Jordan, you and all this people, to the land which I am giving to them, to the sons of Israel.

> Joshua 1:6 Be strong and courageous, for you shall give this people possession of the land which I swore to their fathers to give them.

Here Jehovah indicates his purpose to give Israel the land through Joshua. He also forecasts the day when, having given Israel the land, the soldiers from the tribes who had their inheritance in the land across the Jordan would return to their families in Joshua 1:14-15.

> [14] "Your wives, your little ones, and your cattle shall remain in the land which Moses gave you beyond the Jordan, but you shall cross before your brothers in battle array, all your valiant warriors, and shall help them, [15] until the LORD gives your brothers rest, as *He gives* you, and they also possess the land which the LORD your God is giving them. Then you shall return to your own land, and possess that which Moses the servant of the LORD gave you beyond the Jordan toward the sunrise."

This actually happened later in Joshua 22:4.

> And now the LORD your God has given rest to your brothers, as He spoke to them; therefore turn now and go to your tents, to the land of your possession, which Moses the servant of the LORD gave you beyond the Jordan.

Joshua assumes that God has given Israel the land he promised. Thus, he can threaten them with forfeiture of the land if they sin like in Joshua 23:13-15.

> [13] know with certainty that the LORD your God will not continue to drive these nations out from before you; but they will be a snare and a trap to you, and a whip on your sides and thorns in your eyes, until you perish from off this good land which the LORD your God has given you. [14] "Now behold, today I am going the way of all the earth, and you know in all your hearts and in all your souls that not one word of all the good words which the LORD your God spoke concerning you has failed; all have been fulfilled for you, not one of them has failed. [15] "It shall come about that just as all the good words which the LORD your God spoke to you have come upon you, so the LORD will bring upon you all the threats, until He has destroyed you from off this good land which the LORD your God has given you.

I have labored this point because it is crucial. We must be clear that God's promises were not fulfilled to the generation that originally left Egypt. Only two of those above the age of 20 survived to see the fulfillment of the promise of the land. Yet this is viewed as God keeping His promises to Israel. What is true here in Joshua and of the original generation of the covenant nation is true throughout its history. The promises are fulfilled to the elect remnant. And this counts as fulfilling the promises to the nation. Thus, Judah's dwelling in the land counts as fulfilling the promises of God even when the northern tribes are exiled and lost forever. Thus, the return from exile of the remnant counts as the return of Israel to the land.

Even so Paul's apology in Romans 9-11 is built on this principle of the remnant. The word of God to Israel has not failed (Romans 9:6) because the promises are fulfilled to the elect remnant (Romans 9:7-13). Romans 9:27 emphasizes the point:

> Isaiah cries out concerning Israel, "THOUGH THE NUMBER OF THE SONS OF ISRAEL BE LIKE THE SAND OF THE SEA, IT IS THE REMNANT THAT WILL BE SAVED;

This is also Paul's point in Romans 11. Listen to how Paul starts his argument there.

> Romans 11:1 I say then, God has not rejected His people, has He? May it never be! For I too am an Israelite, a descendant of Abraham, of the tribe of Benjamin.

Paul's point is that his own salvation as a Jew proves that God has not rejected His people. Paul is a Jew, and he is saved. The people corporately or as a nation are saved in the remnant.

Paul also illustrates this idea of the salvation of the corporate people in the remnant from the days of Elijah in Romans 11:2-4.

> [2] God has not rejected His people whom He foreknew. Or do you not know what the Scripture says in *the passage about* Elijah, how he pleads with God against Israel? [3] "Lord, THEY HAVE KILLED YOUR PROPHETS, THEY HAVE TORN DOWN YOUR ALTARS, AND I ALONE AM LEFT, AND THEY ARE SEEKING MY LIFE." [4] But what is the divine response to him? "I HAVE KEPT for Myself SEVEN THOUSAND MEN WHO HAVE NOT BOWED THE KNEE TO BAAL."

From this Paul concludes that the same principle continues to operate in his day. In Romans 11:5, he says, "In the same way then, there has also come to be at the present time a remnant according to *God's* gracious choice."

Throughout the rest of Romans 11 the theme of the fulfillment of God's promises to the nation corporately in the persons of the elect remnant is pursued.

> Romans 11:14 if somehow I might move to jealousy my fellow countrymen and *save some of them.*

> Romans 11:25 For I do not want you, brethren, to be uninformed of this mystery - so that you will not be wise in your own estimation - that *a partial hardening* has happened to Israel until the fullness of the Gentiles has come in;

Even the Isaiah 59:20-21 passage cited by Paul in connection with the much disputed assertion that all Israel will be saved in Romans 11:26 may be seen as emphasizing in its Hebrew original the salvation of the remnant.

> [20] "A Redeemer will come to Zion, *And to those who turn from transgression in Jacob*," declares the LORD. [21] "As for Me, this is My covenant with them," says the LORD: "My Spirit which is upon you, and My words which I have put in your mouth shall not depart from your mouth, nor from the mouth of your offspring, nor from the mouth of your offspring's offspring," says the LORD, "from now and forever."

It is not my purpose here to answer the vexed question of whether there will be a future revival among the Jews. My only purpose is to say that it is not necessary for a whole future generation of Israelites to be saved *en masse* for God to fulfill His promises to Israel. It is not necessary for God to save every member of such a generation or even most of the members of such a generation to keep His promises. God has genuinely and authentically fulfilled those promises many times to the elect remnant. Those promises were never made to any, but that elect remnant of which Paul speaks at length in Romans 9-11.

Here we come back to the main point. The elect remnant of the Jews is now the nucleus of the Christian Church. That elect remnant of the Jews in the Church is God's present fulfillment of His promises to Israel. The Church is and must be the New Israel. Partly because of this elect remnant the whole Church is the seed of Abraham.

CHAPTER EIGHTEEN
Must Israelites be Ethnic Jews?

I realize the question raised in the heading to this chapter will probably strike my Dispensational brethren as outrageous. I do not know for sure if MacArthur was serious, half-serious, or kidding when he spoke of modern Israel having DNA tests for Jewish ethnicity in his message. I do know he thinks that being a physical Jew is essential to be Jewish. Listen to some of his comments on this subject:

> The Bible calls God "The God of Israel" over 200 times--the God of Israel. There are over 2000 references to Israel in Scripture. Not one of them means anything but Israel. Not one of them, including Romans 9:6 and Galatians 6:16, which are the only two passages that Amillennialists go to, to try to convince us that these passages cancel out the other 2000. There is no difficulty in interpreting those as simply meaning Jews who were believers, "the Israel of God." Israel always means Israel; it never means anything but Israel. Seventy-three New Testament uses of Israel always mean Israel. It should be noted that Jews still exist today. That's interesting, isn't it? Have you ever met a Hittite? How about an Amorite, a Hivite, or a Jebusite? Anybody know any of those folks? How about an Agagite?... ...Seventy percent of Scripture is the story of Israel, and I think the whole point of the story is to get to the ending. And it doesn't go up in smoke.

Now, I have already acknowledged that it was necessary for the Church to have an ethnically Jewish Savior. Additionally, I said the Church is built on the ethnically Jewish foundation of the Apostles of Christ. I also affirmed that an ethnically Jewish nucleus in the elect remnant from the nation of Israel was an essential ingredient in the Christian Church. In light of these statements, I am not (in what I am about to say) totally discounting or denying Jewish ethnicity as essential in some way for understanding the Church.

Nevertheless, it is now necessary to state a balancing truth. It is a truth that I think is absolutely devastating for the viewpoint of MacArthur and his sympathizers. *Jewish ethnicity (being descended from ethnically Jewish parents or even one ethnically Jewish parent) was never essential to being a citizen of Israel.* From the beginning, provision was made for the membership of ethnic Gentiles in the Commonwealth of Israel. In the Old Testament, it was possible to receive circumcision and so take upon oneself the blessings and responsibilities of the Abrahamic and Mosaic Covenant. This rite was crucial to Abraham himself who was originally an ethnic Gentile. We are told in Genesis 17:10-12 (and Acts 7:8) that circumcision was the covenant and the sign of the covenant between God, Abraham, and his seed.

> [10] "This is My covenant, which you shall keep, between Me and you and your descendants after you: every male among you shall be circumcised. [11] "And you shall be circumcised in the flesh of your foreskin, and it shall be the sign of the covenant between Me and you. [12] "And every male among you who is eight days old shall be circumcised throughout your generations, a servant who is born in the house or who is bought with money from any foreigner, who is not of your descendants.

We are, therefore, told that both Moses and his children and Israel in the time of Joshua had to be circumcised (Exodus 4:26; Joshua 5:1-8). In conformity with this, provision was later made (with some restrictions) for Gentiles to be circumcised and become members of the QAHAL ISRAEL (Deuteronomy 23:1-9). It was necessary for both ethnic Jews and Gentiles to be circumcised in order to eat the covenant meal–the Passover (Exodus 12:43-48). At the same time, it must also be remembered that since the right of circumcision was crucial to covenant standing no ethnic Jewess could become a part of the church or commonwealth of Israel. Here is another proof that ethnic Jewish-ness (Jewish DNA) was not sufficient to give one standing as a member of Israel. Female Jewish DNA did not suffice.[1]

---

[1] In this connection notice the statement of Esther 8:17, "many among the

But, there is much more to be said to our Dispensational brethren about this. To borrow the words of Revelation 9:12, "The first woe is past; behold, two woes are still coming after these things." Now, it is clear that circumcision was necessary to be a member of Old Testament Israel. But, in the New Covenant, physical circumcision has been abolished and replaced by spiritual circumcision (the circumcision of Christ). In fulfillment of the Old Testament type (Deuteronomy 10:16; 30:6), it is now spiritual circumcision that avails for covenant status. This opens a path of inclusion into the commonwealth of Israel for both women and non-circumcised Gentiles and simultaneously *excludes* even physically circumcised ethnic Jews (Romans 2:25-29; 1 Corinthians 7:18-19; Galatians 5:6; 6:15; Ephesians 2:11-12; Philippians 3:2-3; Colossians 2:11; 3:11). Physical circumcision now counts for nothing. Only spiritual circumcision constitutes one as truly circumcised in God's sight.

So what is the point? The point is that even in the Old Testament it was not merely ethnic Jewish-ness that made one a member of Israel—*it was circumcision*. MacArthur's emphasis on ethnic Jewish-ness is in profound conflict with what the Bible actually teaches concerning what makes a man an Israelite. His emphasis conflicts with the necessity of circumcision, in the Old Testament, for an ethnic Jew to participate in the covenant people. Furthermore, MacArthur's emphasis obscures the ability of circumcision in the Old Testament to grant covenantal rights to ethnic Gentiles who by physical circumcision and the embrace of the covenantal stipulations became Jews. In the New Covenant, physical circumcision has been abolished and replaced by spiritual circumcision. It is now spiritual circumcision that is crucial to covenant status. Consequently, Gentiles and women who believe in Christ (and thus have received the circumcision of Christ) qualify as members of the commonwealth of Israel (Ephesians 2:11-19). If in the Old Testament Gentiles could become true Israelites, they certainly can become members of the commonwealth of Israel in the New Testament by spiritual circumcision.

Much else could be said by way of pointing out the typical, provisional, and temporary character of national Israel in God's

---

peoples of the land became Jews, for the dread of the Jews had fallen on them." Clearly, it was possible in Esther's day for an ethnic Gentile to become a Jew!

plan. It has often been argued, for instance, that the restriction of God's covenant to national Israel always had a universal intention (Genesis 12:3). This is true. What has been said here, however, is sufficient to show that MacArthur's extreme emphasis on ethnic and national Israel in the future plan of God is very misguided.

CHAPTER NINETEEN
The New Testament is the *New Testament*

The history of Dispensational exegesis contains a number of desperate attempts to avoid one of the plainest exegetical features of the New Testament. It is the fact that the New Testament is *the New Testament* or New Covenant. This simple fact (when backed up both by every occurrence of the words "New Covenant" and by every quotation of Jeremiah 31:31-34 in the New Testament) is a gigantic problem that Dispensationalism has never solved. Perhaps, however, I need to explain in more detail what I mean.

What I mean, first, is that the name of the second part of our Bibles and of the Christian Scriptures is New Testament or Covenant. This terminology is indisputably borrowed directly from Jeremiah 31. Now, Classic Dispensationalism argued the New Covenant was future and millennial. Some Dispensationalists even argued that there were two new covenants. Progressive Dispensationalism wants to say there are two fulfillments of the New Covenant–one in the Church age and another in the millennium. Against all such abortive attempts to reconcile Dispensationalism with the very name of the Christian Scriptures stands the incorrigible fact that the Christian Church always has and always will call the second part of its Bible the New Testament. This simple fact refutes Classic Dispensationalism. It refutes the two-new-covenants theory. It even calls into question the two-fulfillment theory of the New Covenant held by Progressive Dispensationalism.

Such refutation becomes even clearer with both the actual usages of the phrase and the actual quotations of Jeremiah 31:31-34 in the New Testament. The following passages clearly allude to Jeremiah 31: Matthew 26:28-29; Mark 14:24-25; Luke 22:20; 1 Corinthians 11:25; 2 Corinthians 3:6; and Hebrews 7:22; 8:7-13; 9:15; 10:16-20;

12:24; 13:20. Many other passages might be cited as alluding to the New Covenant. I do urge the reader to consider many of the other occurrences of "New" and "Covenant" in the New Testament. The above passages are, however, the ones where I think there is an undeniable allusion to Jeremiah 31:31-34.

Now, the fact is that every one of those passages assumes the Church as the people with whom the New Covenant is made. There is not one that alludes to a future millennium. The New Covenant is made with the House of Israel and the House of Judah according to Jeremiah 31. According to the New Testament, it is made with the Church. The natural conclusion is that the Church of Christ is the House of Israel and the House of Judah. As a matter of fact, we have seen that this is exactly what the rest of the New Testament teaches.

The passages listed above supply abundant evidence that this equation of the Church with Israel is correct. According to these texts, the Lord's Supper is an ordinance of the New Covenant. Its cup is the very cup that symbolizes the New Covenant (Luke 22:20; 1 Corinthians 11:25). The Apostle of the Gentiles and of the Church, in the context of describing his own ministry, identifies himself as a minister of the New Covenant (2 Corinthians 3:6). Jesus is called the mediator of the New Covenant in a context which describes the glorious privileges of the Christian Church (Hebrews 12:24). Notwithstanding the excesses of extreme Dispensationalists, the Book of Hebrews is written to Christian Churches with Christian elders (Hebrews 13:7, 17, 24). Furthermore, in Hebrews, all the key institutions of the Mosaic Covenant are said to be fulfilled in the blessings the Church possesses in the New Covenant.

Lastly, it is indisputably clear that in the Church one finds the elect remnant of Israel. They are *physically* the House of Israel and of Judah with whom God promised to make the New Covenant. They must be viewed as fulfilling the promises to the nation. Why? Because Paul argues in Romans 9-11, in an undeniable way, that God is fulfilling His promises to Israel in the elect remnant. With the abolition of physical circumcision, all that is necessary to make a man a new and true Israelite is the blessing of the circumcision of Christ (Romans 2:25-29; Ephesians 2:11-13; Philippians 3:3).

In summary, the whole attempt of Dispensationalism to explain away the New Testament's very designation, as well as its teaching, has been wholly misguided. The need to engage in such a futile endeavor is in itself one of the best proofs of the failure of the system as a whole. The Church is the Israel of God, and it is not necessary to be a spiritualizer to say so.

CHAPTER TWENTY
If the Church is Israel,
Why Doesn't it Inherit Israel's Curses?

In his manifesto, John MacArthur echoes an argument he has used before in favor of Premillennialism. It is the claim that Amillennialists are inconsistent in identifying the Church as Israel because they do not want to attribute Israel's curses to the Church. Rather, they only want to attribute Israel's blessings. Here is what he says:

> It also strikes a strange dichotomy since all the curses promised to Israel came to Israel, not the Church; literally, and they're still coming. If you wondered whether the curses in the Old Testament were literal, they are going on right now. Israel right now is not under divine protection. They are under the promise of God that they will be perpetuated as an ethnic people, but this current group of Jews that live in the world today and in the nation Israel are not now under divine protection. They are apostate. They have rejected their Messiah. They are under divine chastening, but they are still a people and will be to the end. What a staggering apologetic that is for the truthfulness of Scripture. You can't abandon that without a huge loss of confidence in Scripture. All the curses promised to Israel for disobedience to God came true literally on Israel. Now, all of a sudden, are we supposed to split all those passages that give blessing and cursing and say all the blessings that were promised to Israel aren't coming to Israel; they are coming to the Church instead? Where is the textual justification for such a split interpretation? Wouldn't you think that whatever way the curses were fulfilled would set the standard for whatever way the blessings would be fulfilled? Or to put the question in another context, wouldn't you expect that all of the prophecies that came to pass in a literal fashion when Jesus came

the first time would set the pattern for how the prophecies connected to His second coming would come to pass? There is no place for splitting up these interpretations.

This argument is familiar to someone who knows MacArthur.

Now, when Israel sinned, disobeyed God--what happened? Judgment, chastening, cursing, slaughter--was it literal? Yes. Was it Israel? Yes. So if Israel received all of the promised curses-- literally--why would we assume they would not receive the promised blessings literally, because some of those are in the same passages? And how can you say in this passage the cursing means literal Israel, but the blessings means the Church? There is no exegetical basis for that and you now have arbitrarily split the verse in half--you've given all the curses to Israel and all the blessing to the Church--on what basis exegetically?[1]

I understand MacArthur's objection to be really two objections in one. The first objection has to do with the issue of literal interpretation which we have already discussed at length. Substantially, MacArthur argues that Amillennialists are inconsistent in their hermeneutics by viewing the curses as fulfilled on physical Israel, but taking the blessings as fulfilled to the spiritual Israel, the Church. This argumentation, however, assumes that the Church is not really Israel, but only Israel's replacement. I have argued at length, however, that Amillennialists need not hold replacement theology or supersessionism. I have also argued the Church is in a real and even literal sense the reformation and expansion of Israel.

The second aspect of MacArthur's objection is the one that interests me here. The aspect I have in mind is the implicit charge of inconsistency in claiming for the Church Israel's blessings, but not

---

[1] I accessed this on August 2, 2007 from the following website address: http://www.biblebb.com/files/macqa/70-16-9.htm. The answer from which the quotation was taken was preceded by the following explanation: "The following "Question" was asked by a member of the congregation at Grace Community Church in Panorama City, California, and "Answered" by their pastor, John MacArthur Jr. It was transcribed from the tape, GC 70-16, titled "Bible Questions and Answers." A copy of the tape can be obtained by writing, Word of Grace, P.O. Box 4000, Panorama City, CA 91412 or by dialing toll free 1-800-55-GRACE. Copyright John MacArthur Jr., All Rights Reserved."

Israel's curses. MacArthur, I think, is saying: "Hey, fair is fair. You have to take the bad with the good. You can't have your cake and eat it too. If you want Israel's blessings for the Church, you have to take for the Church Israel's curses too." Now, I admit that in a way such an argument has a certain appeal–a plausible sound. At first glance, it does seem both self-serving and inconsistent for Amillennialists to interpret the Bible this way.

But I think the plausibility of this argument disappears when one considers the whole matter in a less superficial and more biblical light. Perhaps the main thing that has to be said is that Amillennialists are not claiming the Church is the same old Israel under the same Old Covenant. Amillennialists are claiming the Church is the New Israel under the New Covenant. Look and you will find no curses for Israel in the New Covenant in Jeremiah 31:31-34. The New Covenant supplies the conditions of the covenant and so insures its blessed fruition for those with whom it is made. Christ is the guarantee of this better covenant (Hebrews 7:22). There are no curses for those who fulfill the conditions of the covenant.

Another way to see this point is to remember that we have said the Church is by definition the elect remnant of Israel (Romans 9:6-13). How can there be curses for God's elect? The head of the Church is the elect Messiah. The foundation stones of the Church (the Apostles) are elect Israelites. The nucleus of the Church consists of those Jews that received with faith their Messiah. There is no curse for the elect remnant.

Remember the one olive tree of Romans 11:1-24? This olive tree is an illustration of the covenant people in the new age. It is, in other words, the New Israel. It is composed of the remaining Jewish, believing branches that are not cut off and of the Gentile, believing branches that are grafted in. There can be no curse for such believers as long as they remain in the one olive tree by faith.

Yet another way to see this is to recognize that the Church is eschatological Israel–the Church of the Messiah or QAHAL MASHIACH. MacArthur himself believes in an eschatological Israel whose lot is blessing and not cursing. All we are saying is that the Church is that eschatological Israel.

So, while it may seem inconsistent to claim the blessings of Israel for the Church and not the curses, when the matter is examined scripturally it is not a problem. Our claim is not that the Church is the same old Israel under the same Old Covenant. Our claim is that the Church is the New Israel under the New Covenant, the elect remnant of Israel, the one olive tree of blessing, and the eschatological Israel which inherits all God's promises. There are really two Israels. There always have been–only the contrast is now clearer. There has always been the external nation and the elect remnant. For the Church–the New, Elect, Believing, Messianic, and Eschatological Israel, God's blessings remain. God's curses are for those external Jews who finally reject their Messiah.

CHAPTER TWENTY-ONE
Of Jewish Evangelism

MacArthur is convinced that eschatology has enormously practical implications. In fact, he closes his message by emphasizing one of these implications. Only his eschatology, he believes, lays a wonderful foundation for Jewish evangelism. He is certain Amillennialism undermines it. Here are some of the closing words of his message:

> Another effect of replacement theology is the damage that it does to Jewish evangelism. Here is a little scenario: You are talking to a Jew. You say, "Jesus is the Messiah." He says, "Really, where is the kingdom?" "Oh, it's here!" "Oh, it is? Well, why are we being killed all the time? Why are we being persecuted and why don't we have the land that was promised to us? And why isn't the Messiah reigning in Jerusalem, and why isn't peace and joy and gladness dominating the world, and why isn't the desert blooming and...?" "Oh, no, you don't understand. All that's not going to happen. You see, the problem is you're not God's people any more. We are." "Oh! I see, but this is the kingdom, and Jews are being killed and hated, and Jerusalem is under siege. This is the kingdom? If this is the kingdom, Jesus is not the Messiah. He can't be. It's ludicrous." No matter how many wonderful Jewish-Christian relationships we try to have with rabbis, this is a huge bone in the throat. Why can't Jesus be the Messiah? Because this isn't the kingdom. Unless you can say to a Jew "God will keep every single promise He made to you, and Jesus will fulfill every single promise, and that is why there are still Jews in the world, and that is why you are in the land and God is preparing for a great day of salvation in Israel; and Jesus is your Messiah. But look at Psalm 22 and Isaiah 53 and Zechariah 12:10 and understand that He had to come and die to ratify the New Covenant before He

could forgive your sin, and the kingdom is coming," you don't
have a chance to communicate! The rest doesn't make sense.

MacArthur is right to be concerned about Jewish evangelism. We
are all in favor of it. May God wonderfully bless our brother's and
his ministry's efforts. Nevertheless, I think there are numerous
difficulties with the way MacArthur uses Jewish evangelism
polemically against Amillennialism in this passage.

First, MacArthur attributes to Amillennialists an over-realized
eschatology. MacArthur reasons, "You are talking to a Jew. You
say, "Jesus is the Messiah." "Really, where is the kingdom?" "Oh,
it's here!" "Oh, it is? Well, why are we being killed all the time?
Why are we being persecuted and why don't we have the land that
was promised to us?"" Here is my response. I would not say these
words to a persecuted Jew. Neither would I say them to a persecuted
Christian. Here I want to remind the reader of the chapter I entitled,
"Not Your Father's Amillennialism." I will hereby admit that some
older Amillennialists may have been guilty of associating the
promised kingdom entirely with the Church age and not with the
coming age. I and most contemporary Amillenialists, however, are
committed to the idea of "the already and not yet" as it has been
developed in recent years by Evangelical theologians. This means
we would never claim that an earth in which Christians are still
being persecuted and killed is God's consummate kingdom. It is the
inaugural phase of the kingdom. In the inaugural phase of the
kingdom Jesus taught that sacrifice and persecution would be facts
of life. Remember the parables of the tares, the treasure hidden in
the field, and the pearl of great price (Matthew 13:24-30, 36-46).

Second, MacArthur assumes Amillennialists believe the Jews
have forfeited all God's promises to them as a nation. He says, "All
that's not going to happen. You see, the problem is you're not God's
people any more. We are." I have argued extensively that this is a
complete misunderstanding of contemporary Amillennialism. Our
position is not that God will not fulfill His promises to the Jews. Our
position is that He is fulfilling those promises right now to those
Jews who embrace the Savior-Messiah. We also hold that a glorious
kingdom awaits such Jews in the age to come. This kingdom will
not be less than what the Jews were promised. It will be infinitely
more than the Old Testament types and shadows could convey. The

meek will not simply inherit the land. They will inherit the earth (Matthew 5:5; Ephesians 6:1-3). A New Jerusalem–much better than the old one–will come down out of heaven from God.

Third, MacArthur assumes Amillennialists have to admit God does not keep His promises to the Jews. He reasons, "Unless you can say to a Jew 'God will keep every single promise He made to you, and Jesus will fulfill every single promise, and that is why there are still Jews in the world, and that is why you are in the land and God is preparing for a great day of salvation in Israel; and Jesus is your Messiah.'" In a sense I have already responded to this reasoning, but something remains to be said. I can say, to the believing Jew or to the Jew on condition of his believing, that God will fulfill every promise He made to them. I have said so again and again in these chapters. But, I can't say any such thing to unbelieving Jews.

Furthermore, the Jews present occupation of their ancient land in itself can be no fulfillment of Scripture's promised return of Israel to the land. The promised return to the land is the return of a repentant people. The earliest promise which Dispensationalists usually quote in this regard is Deuteronomy 30:1-6. It clearly says the promised return is the return of a repentant people:

> [1] "So it shall be when all of these things have come upon you, the blessing and the curse which I have set before you, and you call *them* to mind in all nations where the LORD your God has banished you, [2] and you return to the LORD your God and obey Him with all your heart and soul according to all that I command you today, you and your sons, [3] then the LORD your God will restore you from captivity, and have compassion on you, and will gather you again from all the peoples where the LORD your God has scattered you. [4] "If your outcasts are at the ends of the earth, from there the LORD your God will gather you, and from there He will bring you back. [5] "The LORD your God will bring you into the land which your fathers possessed, and you shall possess it; and He will prosper you and multiply you more than your fathers. [6] "Moreover the LORD your God will circumcise your heart and the heart of your descendants, to love the LORD your God with all your heart and with all your soul, so that you may live.

Obviously, the present Jewish state persecutes Christians, and the mass of its inhabitants do not recognize Jesus as Messiah. It cannot, therefore, be the promised return to the land. This reality is further supported by Jeremiah 31:1-34 and 32:40-44, which reads:

> [40] "I will make an everlasting covenant with them that I will not turn away from them, to do them good; and I will put the fear of Me in their hearts so that they will not turn away from Me. [41] "I will rejoice over them to do them good and will faithfully plant them in this land with all My heart and with all My soul. [42] "For thus says the LORD, 'Just as I brought all this great disaster on this people, so I am going to bring on them all the good that I am promising them. [43] 'Fields will be bought in this land of which you say, "It is a desolation, without man or beast; it is given into the hand of the Chaldeans." [44] 'Men will buy fields for money, sign and seal deeds, and call in witnesses in the land of Benjamin, in the environs of Jerusalem, in the cities of Judah, in the cities of the hill country, in the cities of the lowland and in the cities of the Negev; for I will restore their fortunes,' declares the LORD."

These verses clearly assert that restoration to the land and regeneration are coincident. Now, I do agree with MacArthur on one point. The Jews will continue to exist as a distinct people group. In my view, Romans 11 assumes this. At a number of points I have argued the nucleus of the Church is the elect Jewish remnant. Nevertheless, this does not mean that the modern State of Israel is the commencement of the promised return.

What really gets in the way of Jewish evangelism is communicating to the Jews that they have some sort of inside track with God regardless of their spiritual condition. In my view, saying the land belongs to them regardless of their spiritual condition communicates the wrong thing. Saying to them that the present State of Israel, in spite of their ongoing rejection of the Messiah, has some sort of divine right to the land also communicates the idea that they have some sort of inside track on God's blessings. No matter how much I may support the State of Israel for moral, political, and pragmatic reasons this is completely different from supporting them for theological or prophetic reasons. To communicate that they have some sort of theological or prophetic claim on the land and God's blessings in their impenitent Christ-rejecting condition is not good for their souls. This, I think, is the true danger to Jewish evangelism–not Amillennialism.

CHAPTER TWENTY-TWO
Together for the Gospel?

I attended the first "Together for the Gospel" conference in Louisville, KY (2006) at which MacArthur was one of the speakers. It was a delightful experience. It is certainly a matter of rejoicing to see Evangelical leaders with Reformed leanings from a number of different backgrounds recognizing their commonality and coming together to give united testimony to their fellowship in the Gospel.

Even there in Louisville, in my opinion, MacArthur sounded a somewhat distinctive note with his open references to both election and Premillennialism. Frankly, I appreciated his willingness to be specific and clear with regard to his own doctrinal perspectives–even if I disagreed with him about Premillennialism. Why? There is a danger, of course, in the kind of wonderful Gospel love-fest that was happening there in Louisville. There could be a loss of appreciation for the fact that important doctrinal distinctives might be tossed overboard solely for the purpose of feeling good about each other. Unity is no excuse for doctrinal fuzziness. This made me respond positively to MacArthur's willingness to be specific about his doctrinal beliefs.

But, I can well imagine someone at the Shepherds' Conference (and at other venues where MacArthur has articulated his eschatological views) groaning and wondering out loud: "Should MacArthur make this an issue now? Is Premillennialism a sufficient reason to run the risk of wrecking the ship of unity about a Reformed understanding of the Gospel on the rocks of controversy?" Here I need to say to the person I am imagining (because I do not think he exists only in my imagination) that I am sympathetic. One could well view MacArthur as being unnecessarily "crusty" and "right-angled" for bringing up disputes that merely concern Premillennialism versus Amillennialism in a context like

"Together for the Gospel." This does not mean that I do not hold firmly to Amillennialism as opposed to Premillennialism. But, if this was all that was at stake, then I would agree with my not-so-imaginary groaning friend. I would also want to say to MacArthur, the Gospel is much more important than detailed disputes about prophecy. So, unless this debate is something more important than an intramural discussion among Reformed Christians about the millennium this should not be an issue.

CHAPTER TWENTY-THREE
Of Panmillennialism and Hyper-Preterism

There are, of course, eschatological issues that impact our understanding of the Gospel. We–many of us at least–are accustomed to thinking of eschatology as merely a secondary issue. We have all heard the joke about the Panmillennialist. You know, he's the Christian who tells you light-heartedly that his eschatological view is that everything will "pan out" in the end.

Yet, there are some eschatological disputes that are important enough to bring up in the discussion of issues essential to the Gospel. Here is where I sympathize with MacArthur. MacArthur, without explicitly calling it by name, brings up the issue of Hyper-Preterism. This is the view that all prophecy was fulfilled in A.D. 70 and that Christ came back then, never to return again. I agree that extreme Preterist views do impact our understanding of the Gospel story and should not be glossed over in any "togetherness" for the Gospel. Note Macarthur's concern over hyper-Preterism:

> But let me tell you something, folks, as wacky as that world of Dispensational eschatology can be, it is no more wacky than the interpretation of many Amillennialists whose fictional eisegesis reads everything into 70 A.D. And I've read that kind of stuff and it's just as crazy.

In this context, MacArthur is referring to some of the extremes of popular Dispensationalism. Let me just say, "Amen, John!" to what he says about hyper-Preterism here. In fact, let me say that hyper-Preterism is much worse than the Dispensational extremes he described. At least such extremist Dispensational teachers believe in the Second Coming of Christ. This is more than can be said for hyper-Preterists. Of course, I do take exception to MacArthur identifying such Preterist extremes with Amillennialism. Let me make it clear that as far as I am concerned hyper-Preterism is heresy. I reject it even more emphatically than I reject Dispensationalism. Yet, historically speaking, Preterist views of prophecy, though not hyper-Preterist, have been identified more with Postmillennialism than Amillennialism. But, as we have seen, MacArthur really cannot see the difference between these two views.

So, I feel some sympathy for MacArthur's desire not to shelve the subject of eschatology while attending "Together for the Gospel." The problem is when MacArthur actually raises the eschatological issue he does so in a way that does not carry my judgment, if I take him seriously. Listen to what he says:

> Now at this point, I feel the vibe coming from those of you who are saying, "Oh no, we came to a pastors' conference, and it's turned into a Dispensational conference. Next thing he's going to do is drag out Clarence Larkin charts, and we're going to get a really nice leather-bound Scofield Bible, and then we're all going to get the *Left Behind* series. Ah, we're reduced to rapture fiction. Then he's probably going to tell us there are seven Dispensations, two kingdoms, two new covenants, two ways of salvation. Relax. Forget Dispensationalism. I'm not talking about that, even though every one of you is a Dispensationalist.

As I have previously said, MacArthur appears to distance himself from Dispensationalism in statements like these. In this and other statements he presents himself as merely championing the cause of Premillennialism and not the cause of Dispensationalism. Of course, MacArthur implies that he is a Dispensationalist, but it is clear this is not the issue he wishes to raise. The issue he wishes to raise (he would have us understand) is simply Premillennialism.

MacArthur is, of course, wrong here. In both raising the issues of supersessionism/replacement theology and in denying that the Church is the Israel of God, he has placed himself squarely in the camp of *Dispensational* Premilllennialism. As I have shown, he has actually rejected Historic or Covenant Premillennialism. MacArthur is not, then, simply defending essential Premillennialism. He is asserting a variant modern form of Premillennialism that differs from Historic Premillennialism. Historic Premillennialism actually has more in common with Amillennialism and Postmillennialism than it does with Dispensationalism.

But, let us leave all this aside. If I take MacArthur at face value, if I really accept that his point is simply to defend Premillennialism *per se* and not Dispensational Premillennialism, then I think his injection of this issue into the coming together of Reformed Evangelicals over their common understanding of the Gospel is indefensible. Why do the other Premillennialists involved in this movement not feel the need to raise this issue? It is, I think, because they are not Dispensationalists. They realize that the mere issue of whether Christ comes back before or after the millennium does not radically affect one's understanding of the Gospel or Christianity. I think they are right. Premillennialism (pro or con) need not disrupt the unity of "Together for the Gospel."

CHAPTER TWENTY-FOUR
Is There an Issue in the House?

In my view, Premillennialism only becomes a big enough issue to raise in the context of "Together for the Gospel" when it is understood in its Dispensational form. This is why MacArthur actually feels the need to raise it. What he actually believes and wants to defend is not generic Premillennialism but Dispensationalism. I think I have already proved this in a previous chapter.

Now, let me hasten to reaffirm what I have just implied above. I am not saying that Dispensationalism is heresy. I do believe, however, that it raises very basic issues with regard to the true nature of Christianity and the Gospel. I believe that MacArthur's instincts are right in his perception that these issues are important enough to be raised in the present context.

What is the issue that touches on the Gospel itself in the dispute MacArthur raises? Does he have an issue worth raising now when we are together for the Gospel? While I do credit MacArthur as holding the ancient Gospel of Christ, while I prize his ministry for restoring missing notes in the Gospel in our day, I think beneath the surface of MacArthur's manifesto there is an issue that affects one's whole understanding of the Gospel and of Christianity. It is the issue MacArthur has raised. It is the issue of supersessionism or replacement theology. Inseparable from the accusation of supersessionism against his fellow Evangelicals is a distinctive hermeneutic. Listen to MacArthur's words:

Is the Old Testament Amillennial? First, a note here. It is not legitimate to interpret the Old Testament as secondary to the New Testament as primary. Okay? That's not legitimate. Otherwise, the Old Testament was literally darkness, not light. If you say that the

Old Testament cannot be rightly interpreted apart from the New Testament, then you have denied the perspicuity of the Old Testament, and as Walt Kaiser puts it, "Now you have a canon within a canon." The question must be answered: Does the Old Testament itself propound an Amillennial view? You cannot remove the Old Testament from having a true interpretation on its own and make Old Testament promises relate to the Church, which is by Paul's own statement, a mystery unknown in the past. You cannot, therefore, make the Old Testament unintelligible and irrelevant to the Jewish reader. But the idea that the New Testament is the starting point for understanding the Old Testament is exactly where Amillennialism comes from, reading it back into the Old Testament; and, of course, you damage the perspicuity or the clarity of the sensibility of the Old Testament in and of itself. Such an approach leads to an even more grand kind of spiritualizing that goes beyond just prophetic texts and gives license to spiritualize other things and read New Testament Christian principles back into those texts in the Old Testament where they do not rise from a legitimate interpretation.

It is not my purpose here to dismantle Walt Kaiser's hermeneutical views. I do emphatically disagree with his rejection of what Berkhof calls the theological interpretation of the Bible.[1] I think Kaiser, though he believes in the divine authorship of the Bible, refuses to take it into account in his interpretation of the Old Testament. There is no necessary dichotomy between holding the perspicuity of the Old Testament for its original readers and holding that the New Testament's manner of interpreting the Old Testament is final and authoritative. As in all other doctrinal issues, the Apostles of Christ are the authority on how to interpret the Old Testament. One can see the misguided character of Kaiser's and MacArthur's hermeneutics at this point in the very words quoted above. MacArthur summarizes Kaiser's view at one point by saying, "Otherwise, the Old Testament was literally darkness, not light." Now, without denying the Old Testament was the light of God for His Old Testament people, surely we must balance this affirmation by remembering that the New Testament itself in a number of places describes the Old Testament as a book filled with types and shadows (Colossians

---

[1] Louis Berkhof, *Principles of Biblical Interpretation* (Grand Rapids: Baker, 1950), 133ff.

2:16-17; Hebrews 10:1; 1 Peter 1:10-12). Thus, in a certain way the New Testament does affirm the Old Testament was darkness until fulfilled by Christ and the New Covenant. Hence, we must recognize the New Testament is the final authority on how to interpret a book that was in some sense shadowy and dim.

These issues are connected with MacArthur's charges of supersessionism and replacement theology against Amillennialists. As I have made clear, I reject such charges and believe they misrepresent and distort the real views of Amillennialists, Postmillennialists, and Historic Premillennialists. Yet, while such charges reveal little about our views, they reveal a great deal about MacArthur's views. They reveal he does not regard Christianity or the Christian Church as the fulfillment of the Old Testament. Surely this is an important claim. His accusations reveal that he, along with Dispensationalism, actually believes a future saved generation of Jews, the millennium which they dominate, and the restored temple and animal sacrifices with which they worship God, is the true and final historical fulfillment of the Old Testament. Truly, this is a claim which drastically and basically affects our understanding of Christianity. MacArthur is right to think that such a view is so fundamental it may be raised in the context of our coming together for the Gospel.

At its best such a view of the Old Testament must (and does in Classic Dispensationalism) relegate the Christian Church, built on the foundation of Christ and His Apostles, to a secondary role in the fulfillment of the Old Testament. Even in Progressive Dispensationalism the Church is only one of two different fulfillments of the New Covenant. Both Classic and Progressive Dispensationalism, thus, seriously depreciate the Church of Christ. The Church of Christ is not secondary in God's plan. Nor does it share God's plan with Israel. It is God's New Israel. It is the people *upon whom the ends of the ages have come* (1 Corinthians 10:11). This claim is basic to Christianity. Thus, Paul prays *to God be glory in the church and in Christ Jesus to all generations forever and ever* (Ephesians 3:21). Therefore, it is to the Church that our prayers and toils should be given till toils and cares shall end.

APPENDIX ONE
Romans 11 - What about
the Future of Physical Israel?

One of the most interesting and debated passages in the history of New Testament prophecy is Romans 11. The Zionist movement of the twentieth century, culminating in the establishment of the State of Israel in Palestine in 1948, has only increased interest in this text. One interpreter of Romans 11 has said, "... few dare to deny the likelihood of a special providence toward ethnic Israel in the days of the end time."[1]

Often we have the luxury of allowing a trusted theological tradition to guide us, when we consider difficult passages. Those from a Reformed theological tradition know, for instance, that Hebrews 6:1-8 does not teach that the truly saved can finally fall from grace. Rather, it teaches the perseverance of the saints. In the case of Romans 11, however, even the normally trustworthy Reformed tradition is divided. John Murray[2] and many other Reformed writers favor the view that Romans 11 teaches a future, national conversion of Israel. Other well-known Reformed authors oppose this view. There is no substitute, therefore, for a careful re-examination of the passage.

Two expositions of Romans 11 have been of great help to me in studying this passage. William Hendriksen's, *Israel in Prophecy,*

---

[1] O. Palmer Robertson, "Is There a Distinctive Future for Ethnic Israel in Romans 11?" in *Perspectives on Evangelical Theology,* ed. by Kenneth S. Kantzer and Stanley H. Gundry, (Grand Rapids: Baker Book House, 1979), 209.

[2] John Murray, *The Epistle to the Romans* (Grand Rapids: Eerdmans Publishing Co., 1965) en loc.

especially chapter three, is a very useful study.[3] O. Palmer Robertson, in an article entitled "Is There a Distinctive Future for Ethnic Israel?" has provided what has been for me the most helpful exposition of the chapter. The following treatment owes a great deal to this work. The repeated citations of Robertson are all from this article.

When we come to Romans 11, we must answer the question Robertson raises in his title. *Is there a distinctive future for ethnic Israel?* To put that question another way, *Does Romans 11 teach the future, national conversion of Israel?* Robertson is right when he says that two issues must be examined to answer this question. First, we must examine the evidence that Romans 11 deals with God's *present* intention for ethnic Israel. Then, we must examine possible references in Romans 11 to God's intention to deal distinctively with ethnic Israel in the future.

Evidence that Romans 11 deals with God's Present Intention for Ethnic Israel

Here Robertson collects evidence that Romans 11 is dealing with God's present intention for ethnic Israel. This evidence is relevant in that it undermines the idea that the theme of Romans 11 is how God will deal with Israel in the future. Listen to Robertson at this point:

> Most commentators are aware of the references in Romans 11 to God's current saving activity among the Jews. However, the pervasiveness of these references as well as their significance for the total thrust of the chapter, generally is overlooked.

Robertson then shows how Paul, throughout the chapter, continually has reference to God's present dealings with the Jews.

The first part of the chapter is verses 1-10. It begins with the question: "God has not rejected His people, has He?" Paul answers this by speaking not of God's future plans for, but of His present dealings with the Jews. Notice the response in verse 1 to this question, "I too am an Israelite!" Notice also the emphasis of verse

---

[3] William Hendriksen, *Israel in Prophecy* (Grand Rapids: Baker Book House, 1981).

5, "In the same way then, there has also come to be at the present time a remnant according to God's gracious choice."

The second part of the chapter is verses 11-16. Here, too, the emphasis is found on God's present dealings with the Jews. Notice Romans 11:13-14.

> [13] But I am speaking to you who are Gentiles. Inasmuch then as I am an apostle of Gentiles, I magnify my ministry, [14] if somehow I might move to jealousy my fellow countrymen and save some of them.

The third part of the chapter is verses 17-24. There is no reason to postpone the grafting in of the Jews to some future date. The grafting in of the unbelieving Jew takes place whenever he ceases to continue in his unbelief.

The fourth part of the chapter is verses 25-32. This is the last part of the chapter before Paul comes to his doxology in verses 33-36. The emphasis here remains on God's present dealing with the Jews. Romans 11:30 and 31 emphasize that *now* is the time of which Paul is speaking by using that word three times.

> [30] For just as you once were disobedient to God, but *now* have been shown mercy because of their disobedience, [31] so these also *now* have been disobedient, in order that because of the mercy shown to you they also may *now* be shown mercy. (Emphases added.)

Robertson's conclusion is most proper:

> The point originally indicated may be reiterated. Neither the pervasiveness in Romans 11 of references to God's present intention for Israel nor the significance of these references for the total thrust of the chapter has been noted adequately. These references do not exclude by necessity parallel references to some future purpose of God with Israel. They do, however, warn the exegete against assuming too hastily that the entirety of Roman's 11 deals with Israel's distinctive future. Even further, the presence of references to the present role of Israel in every major section of the chapter indicates that the exegete must take into account the significance in Paul's thinking on this present role of Israel,

regardless of the particular section of the chapter under consideration.

To sum up, Paul's reference to the present dealings of God with Israel permeate Romans 11. They are present in every part of the chapter. Interpreters have often neglected this fact. This neglect raises the question as to whether the same interpreters have also misunderstood the supposed references to a future, national conversion of Israel.

Possible References in Romans 11 to God's Intention to Deal Distinctively with Ethnic Israel in the Future

If references to God's present dealings with Israel have been ignored, possible references to a distinctive dealing with Israel in the future have been the primary focus of many expositions of this chapter. Four such references are said to be found in Romans 11. I will give the possible reference and then some pertinent comments.

(1) Romans 11:1 has often been understood to imply a future restoration of the nation of Israel. Paul's question, "God has not rejected His people, has He?" is assumed to mean, "God has not rejected Israel with regard to His special plan for their future, has He?" Once this meaning is assumed then Paul's response, "May it never be!" is seen as a strong affirmation that God has a special plan for Israel's future.

Yet, the context of this question leads us to interpret it in a completely different way. This different way of understanding the question has no reference to a supposed future restoration of the nation of Israel. Paul's question does not mean, "Has God cast off His people finally?" It actually means "Has God cast off His people completely?" In other words, in light of their heinous sin of crucifying the Messiah, Paul now asks, "Is there any hope for them at all? Have they stumbled so as to completely fall?" (Romans 11:11).

Paul's response confirms this is the thrust of his question. His answer is not about the future of Israel, but about their present situation. In verse 1 he says, "I too am an Israelite." In verse 5 he notes, "...there has also come to be at the present time a remnant according to God's gracious choice." Thus, Paul's answer to his question is not that God has a glorious future in store for the nation of Israel. Rather, he answers that God has an elect remnant right now in the nation of Israel. There is no hint of a future, national conversion of Israel in Romans 11:1.

(2) Romans 11:12 and 15 also seem to some to refer to a distinctive future for ethnic Israel.

> [12] Now if their transgression be riches for the world and their failure be riches for the Gentiles, how much more will their fulfillment be! .... [15] For if their rejection be the reconciliation of the world, what will *their* acceptance be but life from the dead?

Those who understand these verses to refer to a future conversion of Israel as a nation assume the transgression, failure, and rejection of the Jews coincides with the present, gospel age, while their fulfillment and acceptance relates to the future period of their national conversion. This assumption is, however, unnecessary. Both can be viewed as taking place during the present gospel age. Robertson remarks:

> The Jews reject their Messiah; the Gentiles believe; the Jews are provoked by jealousy and return in faith; the world receives even richer blessing as consequence of this return of the Jews. ....this temporal sequence may be viewed as having fulfillment in the present era of gospel proclamation.

This alternative understanding of the fulfillment and acceptance of Israel is confirmed by Romans 11:13 and 14:

> [13] But I am speaking to you who are Gentiles. Inasmuch then as I am an apostle of Gentiles, I magnify my ministry, [14] if somehow I might move to jealousy my fellow countrymen and save some of them.

Paul explicitly states his purpose for saying these things. By his own ministry, Paul seeks to save some of the Jews. This certainly suggests their acceptance and fulfillment is not a future, but a present reality already taking place in Paul's day.

(3) Romans 11:17-24 is sometimes taken as implying a future conversion of the Jewish nation. The assumption of this position is that the grafting in of the natural branches (vv. 23-24) takes place

some time in the future. This assumption contradicts, however, the plain teaching of the passage. Paul explicitly says, "And they also, if they do not continue in their unbelief, will be grafted in." There is nothing to suggest this grafting waits for the distant future. Everything in these verses makes clear they would be grafted in when they believe. Note especially Romans 11:20 and 21:

> [20] Quite right, they were broken off for their unbelief, but you stand by your faith. Do not be conceited, but fear; [21] for if God did not spare the natural branches, neither will He spare you.

Parallel passages in the New Testament show that the moment a person believes he begins to partake in the rich root of the olive tree. This is to say, he begins to enjoy the wonderful covenant blessings promised to Israel (Ephesians 2:12-18).

(4) Romans 11:25 and 26 are (supposedly) the most important evidence for a future, glorious conversion of the nation of Israel:

> [25] For I do not want you, brethren, to be uninformed of this mystery, lest you be wise in your own estimation, that a partial hardening has happened to Israel until the fullness of the Gentiles has come in; [26] and thus all Israel will be saved; just as it is written, "THE DELIVERER WILL COME FROM ZION, HE WILL REMOVE UNGODLINESS FROM JACOB."

There are three statements in these verses that are thought to anchor the argument for a distinctive future for ethnic Israel.

1. A partial hardening has happened to Israel.

This is sometimes interpreted to mean for a while hardening has happened to Israel. There is no certain evidence that the Greek phrase in question ever means for a while. The translation of the NASB is certainly correct. The phrase in question means a partial hardening not a hardening for a while.

2. Hardening …until the fullness of the Gentiles has come in

Readers of this passage often assume this indicates the partial hardening will cease after the fullness of the Gentiles come in. Then, they continue to assume, there will be a glorious, national conversion of Israel. All this is based on the weight or meaning to be given to the word, 'until.' This interpretation of 'until' is, however, highly questionable for two reasons.

First, the idea that a partial hardening of Israel would one day cease is highly unlikely. Hardening in the Scriptures has to do with the mystery of election. Romans 11:7 declares, "What then? That which Israel is seeking for, it has not obtained, but those who were chosen obtained it, and the rest were hardened." There are two types of people from the standpoint of election, the chosen and the hardened. The chosen are saved. The hardened are lost. Thus, to say the partial hardening of Israel will one day cease is to assert that the day is coming when every living Israelite will be elect. Even most defenders of a future, national conversion of Israel would not want to say that.

Second, and even more importantly, the precise force of 'until' in Romans 11:25 does not imply the cessation of the partial hardening after the fullness of the Gentiles come in. Robertson says:

> The phrase brings matters "up to" a certain point, or "until" a certain goal is reached. The phrase does not determine in itself the precise state of affairs after the termination. This circumstance can be learned only by the context in which the phrase is used.

In many cases in the Scriptures 'until' has a finalizing meaning. In other words, the idea of 'until' is that a certain condition continues as far as possible or right to the end. Note the following uses of the term in question:

> Acts 22:4 "And I persecuted this Way *to* the death, binding and putting both men and women into prisons,

> Hebrews 4:12 For the word of God is living and active and sharper than any two-edged sword, and piercing *as far as* the division of soul and spirit, of both joints and marrow, and able to judge the thoughts and intentions of the heart.

> 1 Corinthians 15:25 For He must reign *until* He has put all His enemies under His feet.

The idea in Acts 22:4 is not that Paul ceased to persecute people after they died. It is that he persecuted them right up until they died. The idea in Hebrews 4:12 is not that the Word of God only pierced as far as the division of soul and spirit. Rather, it has pierced to the deepest level possible. The idea in 1 Corinthians 15:25 is not that Christ reigns only until all His enemies are defeated, but rather that He reigns right up until they are defeated. As a matter of fact, Christ does not cease to reign when they are defeated. So also in Romans 11:25 the idea is the partial hardening of Israel continues right up until the fullness of the Gentiles come in–at which point Jesus returns. There is no implication that the partial hardening ceases after the fullness of the Gentiles come in.

3. And thus all Israel will be saved

Notice first of all what Paul does not say. He does not say, "And *then* all Israel will be saved." This is the way people often read the text, but the NASB properly reflects the Greek word. Paul does not say "and then" but "and thus." Robertson affirms:

> Immediately prevalent false impressions concerning the weight of this phrase must be removed. Generally the passage is read as though it were saying: "And then all Israel shall be saved." .... However, it is rather difficult to support this rendering of the phrase ... simply because the phrase does not mean "and then." Instead, it means "and in this manner" or "and in this way." Of the approximately 205 times in which the term occurs in the NT, the lexicon of Arndt and Gingrich does not cite a single instance to support the concept of temporal significance.

Thus, when Paul says, "And thus all Israel will be saved," his eye is not looking toward the end of the age. His eye is rather sweeping the entire Gospel age. He sees an elect remnant of Israel saved in every generation. Commenting on this vision he says, "and thus all Israel will be saved." Robertson puts it this way:

> Paul does not look prospectively into the future beyond the "fullness of the Gentiles." Instead, he looks retrospectively into the past. He recalls to the mind of his readers the fantastic processes of God's salvation among the Jews as he has just described them. In accordance with the pattern outlined in the previous verses of

Romans 11, "all Israel shall be saved." First the promises as well as the Messiah were given to Israel. Then, somehow in God's mysterious plan, Israel rejected its Messiah and was cut off from its position of distinctive privilege. As a result, the coming of Israel's Messiah was announced to the Gentiles. The nations then obtained by faith what Israel could not find by seeking in the strength of their own flesh. Frustrated over seeing the blessings of their messianic kingdom heaped on the Gentiles, Israel is moved to jealousy. Consequently they too repent, believe, and share in the promises originally made to them. "And in this manner," by such a fantastic process which shall continue throughout the entire present age "up to" ... the point that the full number of the Gentiles is brought in, all Israel shall be saved.

This exposition of verse 26a leads directly to the question: What does Paul mean by "all Israel?" Robertson distinguishes five possibilities.

(1) "all Israel" refers to all ethnic descendants of Abraham; (2) "all Israel" refers to all ethnic descendants of Abraham living at a future time at which God shall initiate a special working among the Jews; (3) "all Israel" refers to the "mass" or "majority" of Jews living at the time of a special saving activity of God in the future; (4) "all Israel" refers to all the elect Israelites within the community of Israel; (5) "all Israel" refers both to Jews and Gentiles which together constitute the church of Christ, the Israel of God.

The exposition given above enables us to choose with comparative ease from among these alternatives. The first three are variants of the same perspective. As to (1), the idea that all the ethnic descendants of Abraham who have ever lived will one day be saved is so radically unbiblical that few will seek to defend it, if any. As to (2), the idea that all the Israelites living at a future time will be saved is also so extreme that few will wish to assert it. As to (3), the idea that "all Israel" refers to the mass of Jews living at a future time is the most apparently acceptable variant of this perspective. There are still, however, two problems with it. First, this view holds the partial hardening of the Jews is one day lifted. As we have seen, the lifting of the partial hardening entails the idea that all Israelites after that point are elect. So, this view contradicts itself. Second, and more importantly, we have seen that Paul is not surveying the end of the age, but the entire age when he says, thus all Israel shall be saved. It is the collective remnant from every generation which constitutes the "all Israel" of which he speaks. As to (5) then, the idea that "all Israel" is simply the elect from both the Jews and the Gentiles cannot be correct. This view is, of course, possible in the abstract. Nevertheless, in Romans 9-11, and especially in Romans 11, the term 'Israel' has consistently been used to refer to ethnic Israel. It would be improper, then, in such a context to attribute a different meaning to Israel in Romans 11:26.

Alternative (4) must be the right answer. "All Israel" refers to all the elect in every generation from ethnic Israel. Paul sweeps together the remnant of elect Israelites in every generation into "all Israel" in verse 26. Together with the "fullness of the Gentiles," "all Israel" makes up the elect people of God.

Conclusion

Romans 11 does not teach a great, future revival among the Jews. It does, however, contain two points of prophetic interest regarding ethnic Israel. First, it teaches a remnant of Jews will be saved in every generation. Second, it assumes by this the Jews will continue to exist as a distinct, ethnic entity until Jesus return.

APPENDIX TWO

Shepherds' Conference 2007 First Message
Why Every Self-Respecting Calvinist is a Premillennialist
by John MacArthur
(MacArthur's Millennial Manifesto)

Note: Parts of this transcript have been edited for the sake of clarification, readability, and flow. It is reprinted here by permission.

This morning I am not going to preach a sermon. I have a deep concern in my heart that I want to unload on you. I don't want you to take it personally; it is not an attack on anybody. It's just a concern that I've had for a long time for a beloved area of Scripture that I think needs far more careful attention than it has been given. So I want to speak on sovereign election, Israel and eschatology.

That's not the title; that's just the subject. And I want to begin with a sentence that I am going to read to you. It's a very long sentence so don't hold your breath waiting for a period.

It is one of the strange ironies in the Church and in Reformed theology that those who love the doctrine of sovereign election most supremely and most sincerely, and who are most unwavering in their devotion to the glory of God, the honor of Christ, the work of the Spirit in regeneration and sanctification, the veracity and inerrancy of Scripture, and who are the most fastidious in hermeneutics, and who are the most careful and intentionally biblical regarding categories of doctrine, and who see themselves as guardians of biblical truth and are not content to be wrong at all, and who agree most heartily on the essential matters of Christian truth so they labor with all their powers to examine in a Berean fashion every relevant text to discern the true interpretation of all matters of divine revelation, are—that's the main verb—in varying degrees of disinterest in applying those passions and skills to the end of the story and rather content to be in a happy and even playful disagreement in regard to the vast biblical data on eschatology as if the end didn't matter much. Period.

Or, another way to say it would be how many of you have attended an Amill prophecy conference? [Laughter from audience] Or maybe we could say it this way: What other category of theology starts with the alpha privative and labels itself as believing that something does not exist, unless it's atheism?

Does the end matter? Does it matter to God? Should it matter to us? I'm sure it matters to God. I'm sure it's the whole point of history. I *know* it's the whole point of history. History is headed to a divinely designed and revealed end, and if it matters enough to God to reveal it, it should matter enough to us to understand the revelation of it.

Did not God fill Scripture with end time prophecies? Some say that nearly one-fourth of Scripture relates to the prophecies of the end. Did God in this significant volume of revelation somehow muddle His words so hopelessly that the high ground for theologians is simply to recognize the muddle and abandon any thought of the perspicuity of Scripture with regard to eschatology? Is in fact working hard to understand prophetic passages needless, even impossible, because they require a spiritualized or allegorized set of interpretations that says the truth is somehow hidden behind the normal meaning of the words so any idea of what it might mean is as good as any other idea of what it might mean since it doesn't mean what it says?

Are you comfortable with the notion that the hard and fast, tried and true principles of interpretation have to be set aside every time you come to a prophetic text? There are a number of Amillennialists who feel that way; and, by the way, we will talk just in broad terms about Amillennialism. (If any Postmillennialists are left out, you can simply attach to yourself the new label for Postmillennialism which is "optimistic Amillennialism" because the two positions are basically the same. Whether you are a Postmillennialist or an

Amillennialist, you are saying that the kingdom, as identified in the Old Testament and promised to Israel, will not happen. You are either saying that the kingdom will never be literally on earth [Amill] or that it will be replaced by another kind of kingdom which will take place on earth [Postmill]. In either case, you are denying the literal fulfillment of the promised kingdom to Israel.)

O. T. Allis, a well-known Amillennialist, writing in *Prophecy and the Church* says, "The Old Testament prophecies, if literally interpreted, cannot be regarded as having been yet fulfilled or being capable of fulfillment in the present age." That was a problem for him.

Floyd Hamilton in *The Basis of the Millennial Faith* said, "Now we must frankly admit that a literal interpretation of the Old Testament prophecies gives us just such a picture of an earthly reign of the Messiah as the Premillennialist pictures." That was unacceptable to him, thus he called for changing the rules of interpretation when it came to prophecy.

Another Amillennialist, Loraine Boettner in *The Meaning of the Millennium*, said, "It is generally agreed that if the prophecies are taken literally, that they do foretell a restoration of the nation of Israel in the land of Palestine with the Jews having a prominent place in that kingdom and ruling over the other nations."

In all three cases, that proved to them to be a serious problem and required a severe alteration in hermeneutics at each of those prophetic passages in order to avoid a Premillennial conclusion, a fate worse than death. [Laughter from audience] So, to protect a preconception it is necessary to change the rules of interpretation. Now if we're going to change those rules, I think we need a word from God. We better have a word from God because He cares that we get it right.

I don't think God wants us to change the rules of interpretation when we go to Genesis 1–3. I don't think God is pleased when we come up with progressive creationism, theistic evolution or any kind of day-age view of Genesis 1–3. Rather, God is exalted as the Creator in the full glory of His creative power when we take Genesis 1–3 at face value. There is no other way to take it because there is nothing in the text that gives any kind of mandate to indicate that this is something other than specific, literal, normal, factual language. Really you can't even justify calling it poetry because that

doesn't work. Recent studies conducted by one of our professors at
The Master's College, reducing the Creation account linguistically
to a computer program and graphing the comparison between prose
and poetry, led to the very interesting conclusion—that there is
99.9% evidence that this is prose and no possibility that it is poetry.

We don't want anybody tampering with the beginning. Why are
we so tolerant of people tampering with the end? And why, when we
don't want to arbitrarily allow somebody to introduce their own
hermeneutics to Genesis 1–3, are we content to allow people to
introduce their own hermeneutics into prophetic passages
throughout the Bible and particularly in the Book of Revelation?
Where is the divine mandate on the pages of the Bible to do this?
What passage is it in? What verse? Where is it? And who decides
then the new rules for engagement?

Now, back to the original sentence. The irony is that those who
most celebrate the sovereign grace of election regarding the Church
and its inviolable place in God's purpose from predestination to
glorification, and those who most aggressively and militantly defend
the truth of promise and fulfillment, those who are the advocates of
election being divine, unilateral, unconditional and irrevocable by
nature for the Church, unashamedly deny the same for elect Israel.
That is a strange division. As it does, the perpetuity of the elect
Church to salvation glory, so the Scripture in similar language and
by promises

The same God affirms the perpetuity of ethnic Israel to a future
salvation of a generation of Jews that will fulfill all divine promises
given to them by God. In both cases this is the work of and the result
of divine, sovereign election.

Now, that leads to my title: "Why Every Self-Respecting
Calvinist is a Premillennialist." Now it's too late for Calvin, but it's
not too late for the rest of you. [Laughter from audience] And if
Calvin were here, he would join our movement. [More laughter] But
bottom line here, of all people on the planet to be Premillennialist, it
should be Calvinists, those who love sovereign election. Let's leave
Amillennialism for the Arminians. It's perfect. It's ideal. It's a no-
brainer. God elects nobody and preserves nobody. Perfect.
Arminians make great Amillennialists. It's consistent. But not for
those who live and breathe the rarified air of sovereign, electing
grace. That makes no sense. We can leave Amillennialism to the

process theologians or the openness people who think God is becoming what He will be; and He's getting better because as every day goes by, He gets more information; and as He gets more information, He's figuring out whether or not, in fact, He can keep some of the promises He made without having to adjust all of them based upon lack of information when He originally made them. Let's leave Amillennialism to the Charismatics and the semi-Pelagians and other sorts who go in and out of salvation willy-nilly; it makes sense for their theology. Sure, Israel sinned, became apostate, killed the Son of God. That's it. Israel's out and forfeits everything. The church gets it all *if* she can do better than Israel. So far it doesn't look real hopeful.

But for those of us who get it, that God is sovereign and that He is the only one who can determine who will be saved and when they will be saved, and He is the only one who can save them, Amillennialism makes no sense because it basically says Israel, on its own, forfeited all the promises. Do you think, on their own, they could've done something to guarantee they'd receive them? What kind of theology is that? That's Arminian theology. Do you think Israel lost its place in God's economy because the Jews, on their own, didn't do what they were supposed to do?

When we look at the great reality of election in the Bible, there are only four specific persons that are mentioned in regard to being elect. The holy angels are elect—1 Timothy 5:21, "the elect angels." Christ is elect—Isaiah 42 and 1 Peter 2:6. Christ is elect and those elections are forever, are they not? And there are only two people [groups of human beings] elections in Scripture: Israel (an eschatological group of ethnic Israelites that will constitute the future nation who will receive the promises of God) and the Church. There's no reason in the Bible to mingle the two; or because the Church is elect, therefore, cancel Israel's election. Isaiah 45:4 calls Israel "My elect." God says, "For Jacob My servant's sake, and Israel My elect, I have even called thee by thy name." Isaiah 65:9 again calls Israel "My elect" and states that they will inherit the promise. Isaiah 65:22 says the same thing, "My elect." God has repeated it a number of times—those are just a few—that Israel is God's elect.

Now all of that leads us to this: If you get Israel right, you will get eschatology right. If you don't get Israel right, you will never get eschatology right—never. And you will migrate from one view to another just depending on the last book you read or the last lecture you heard or the last influence that came down. If you get eschatology right, it is because you get Israel right. You get Israel right when you get the Old Testament covenants and promises right. Reversing it, you get the Old Testament covenants and promises right when you get the interpretation of Scripture right. You get the interpretation of Scripture right when you're faithful to a legitimate hermeneutic, and God's integrity is upheld. Get your hermeneutics right, and you'll get the Old Testament promises right. Get the promises right, and you'll get Israel right. Get Israel right, and you'll get eschatology right.

The Bible calls God "The God of Israel" over 200 times—the God of Israel. There are over 2000 references to Israel in Scripture. Not one of them means anything but Israel. Not one of them, including Romans 9:6 and Galatians 6:16, which are the only two passages that Amillennialists go to, to try to convince us that these passages cancel out the other 2000. There is no difficulty in interpreting those as simply meaning Jews who were believers, "the Israel of God." Israel always means Israel; it never means anything but Israel. Seventy-three New Testament uses of Israel always mean Israel.

It should be noted that Jews still exist today. That's interesting, isn't it? Have you ever met a Hittite? How about an Amorite, a Hivite, or a Jebusite? Anybody know any of those folks? How about an Agagite? ... Somebody once asked John Stott at a European conference, "What is the significance of the existence of Israel today?" and he replied, "It has no biblical significance." Really? That's a strange answer. They're here. Seventy percent of Scripture is the story of Israel, and I think that the whole point of the story is to get to the ending. And it doesn't go up in smoke.

So, here's how to get the foundation for an accurate understanding of eschatology. Get election right and get Israel right. Those two go together, they're inseparable. How is it that we have come to get number one right and so often miss number two? I'm confident that God did not reveal prophetic truth in such detail to hide or obscure the truth, but to open it for our blessing, our motivation and ultimately His glory.

So, my words to you today are really a call. This is a call to reconnect these two great realities. Return the sovereignty of God in election to its rightful place and, therefore, return the nation Israel to its rightful place in God's purpose, and all eschatology will unfold with magnificent beauty. With the normal hermeneutic [applied consistently], you can interpret every passage and when it's saying something that's very clear like "the desert will blossom like a rose," you can be confident that's exactly what it means. And if you tell me it doesn't mean that, then I'm done listening to your interpretation because you don't have any further revelation [to verify that interpretation].

Now that the Spirit of God is moving the Church to reestablish the glorious high ground of sovereign grace in salvation, it is time to reestablish the equally high ground of sovereign grace for a future generation of ethnic Israel in salvation and the Messianic earthly kingdom, with the complete fulfillment of all God's promises to Israel.

Now, if I can be personal for a minute, I've thought about these great realities for almost fifty years, and the clearer I understand sovereign, electing grace, the clearer the place of Israel becomes to me and the clearer eschatology gets. I haven't moved away. People have said, "Have you changed your eschatology?" I have not moved away from the biblical eschatology I was convinced of when I began. My *ordo eschaton* hasn't changed. This is very encouraging to me because one of the benefits of being in this church for nearly forty years is that I have to keep moving. I can't preach old sermons. These dear people—can you imagine hearing the same preacher for almost forty years? What a death sentence! [Laughter from audience] Not so good for them, but really good for me because I basically have had to continually teach the Bible just to keep moving. I'm getting close to the end of Luke—that's a relative idea—then I only have Mark left.

For forty years I have taught and preached through every verse, every phrase, and every word in the New Testament. I've gone back and written commentaries and books on it. I've preached one verse at a time through every single verse of the New Testament. All I have left, as I said, is a little bit of Luke and then I plan to preach through Mark. Through all of this, eschatology has had to stand the test of every New Testament verse. And my conviction has been strengthened.

I've preached through many Old Testament books, such as Genesis and other sections [of the Old Testament] early in the years here. I started in Genesis [on Wednesday nights] and went kind of rapidly for a number of years, ending up in Psalm 73 before I passed off the opportunity on Wednesday nights to some of the other men who were here. I have preached through the prophetic books of the Old Testament. I've preached in and out of Isaiah and Ezekiel. I've preached through Daniel verse by verse, through Zechariah, and through the Minor Prophets. I've written all the notes for the study Bible, and again, the fair test of a cohesive eschatology is to drag it through every single text. I would be absolutely lost in the Old Testament if I couldn't take the Scripture at its face value. If you tell me it doesn't mean what it says, I'm lost. I am unwaveringly committed to the sovereign election of a future generation of Jews to salvation and the full inheritance of all the promises and covenants of God given to them in the Old Testament because the truth of God's Word is at stake.

Now at this point, I feel the vibe coming from those of you who are saying, "Oh no, we came to a pastors' conference, and it's turned into a Dispensational conference. Next thing he's going to do is drag out Clarence Larkin charts, and we're going to get a really nice leather-bound Scofield Bible, and then we're all going to get the *Left Behind* series. Ah, we're reduced to rapture fiction. Then he's probably going to tell us there are seven Dispensations, two kingdoms, two new covenants, two ways of salvation. Relax. [Laughter from audience]

Forget Dispensationalism. I'm not talking about that, even though every one of you is a Dispensationalist. You are! You believe that God dealt with man one way before the fall, after the fall, before the Law, after the Law, before the Cross, after the Cross, now and in eternity, right? Okay, that's what I thought. [Laughter from audience] I confess I reject the wacky world of newspaper exegesis. I reject the cartoon eschatology: the crazy interpretations like the locusts of Revelation 9 being helicopters and crazy things like that. If you preach that, take that out of the tape. . . .

But let me tell you something, folks, as wacky as that world of Dispensational eschatology can be, it is no more wacky than the interpretation of many Amillennialists whose fictional eisegesis reads everything into 70 A.D. And I've read that kind of stuff and it's just as crazy. You say, well, didn't the Dispensationalists invent Premillennialism? Well, in the modern era two books really reintroduced Premillennial views—the straightforward biblical view—and neither of them were written by a Dispensationalist. The first one was called *The Premillennial Advent*. It was written in 1815 by an Anglican named William Cunningham. The second one that reintroduced this into the more modern era was a publication in England in 1827 written by Emmanuel de Lacunza y Diaz; a Jesuit. So there is not a necessary connection between all that is strange in Dispensationalism and this clear understanding of the kingdom. When Frederick the Great asked his chaplain for proof of the truthfulness of the Bible, he said, "Give me a brief defense." His chaplain replied, "I can do it in one word. *Israel*." Israel. The Jews exist as a people preserved. There they are. Israel, understood as a people preserved by God for an eschatological kingdom, has immense apologetic value. The nation helps us to get the whole counsel of God right. We have to give the world the truth about the end of history and the climactic glory of Christ and the fulfillment of God's promises to Israel and the Church.

So let's get started. That was just the introduction. [Laughter from audience] I'm going to ask you a series of questions, starting with: *Is the Old Testament Amillennial?* First, a note here. It is not legitimate to interpret the Old Testament as secondary to the New Testament as primary. Okay? That's not legitimate. Otherwise, the Old Testament was darkness, not light. If you say that the Old Testament cannot be rightly interpreted apart from the New Testament, then you have denied the perspicuity of the Old Testament, and as Walt Kaiser puts it, "Now you have a canon within a canon." The question must be answered: Does the Old Testament itself propound an Amillennial view? You cannot remove the Old Testament from having a true interpretation on its own and make Old Testament promises relate to the Church, which is by Paul's own statement, a mystery unknown in the past. You cannot, therefore, make the Old Testament unintelligible and irrelevant to the Jewish reader. But the idea that the New Testament is the starting point for understanding the Old Testament is exactly where Amillennialism comes from, reading it back into the Old Testament;

and, of course, you damage the perspicuity or the clarity of the sensibility of the Old Testament in and of itself. Such an approach leads to an even more grand kind of spiritualizing that goes beyond just prophetic texts and gives license to spiritualize other things and to read New Testament Christian principles back into those texts in the Old Testament where they do not rise from a legitimate interpretation.

Some of you have read in years past *If I Perish, I Perish*, the wacky Christian life interpretation of Esther, or a series I talked about in one of my books on Nehemiah where Nehemiah is the Holy Spirit and the fallen walls of Jerusalem are the fallen walls of human heart; and the Lord wants to rebuild your fallen heart by the use of mortar, and mortar is speaking in tongues. [Laughter from audience] That was a six or eight tape series I listened to. But why not? If that's your New Testament theology, then (according to some) you have every right to read it in wherever you want.

This goes on all the time. Honestly, I rarely hear somebody preach on the Old Testament and interpret the Old Testament the way a person living at the time it was written would have interpreted it. We can use it as an illustration; we can use it to elucidate it; we can use it as an example. These things are written as examples, Paul told the Corinthians. But it has to have its own meaning to its own people. It must have clarity and perspicuity. And if you say all those promises to Israel really were to the Church, then they were meaningless and unintelligible to them [the Jews]. Replacement theology is what this is called, by the way, and scholastics often refer to it as supersessionism. It demands that the Old Testament promises be viewed through the lens of the New Testament [such that the Church replaces Israel].

It also strikes a strange dichotomy since all the curses promised to Israel came to Israel, not the Church; literally, and they're still coming. If you wondered whether the curses in the Old Testament were literal, they are going on right now. Israel right now is not under divine protection. They are under the promise of God that they will be perpetuated as an ethnic people, but this current group of Jews that live in the world today and in the nation Israel are not now under divine protection. They are apostate. They have rejected their Messiah. They are under divine chastening, but they are still a people and will be to the end. What a staggering apologetic that is for the truthfulness of Scripture. You can't abandon that without a huge loss of confidence in Scripture. All the curses promised to Israel for disobedience to God came true literally on Israel. Now, all of a sudden, are we supposed to split all those passages that give blessing and cursing and say that all the blessings that were promised to Israel aren't coming to Israel; they are coming to the Church instead? Where is the textual justification for such a split interpretation? Wouldn't you think that whatever way the curses were fulfilled would set the standard for whatever way the blessings would be fulfilled? Or to put the question in another context, wouldn't you expect that all of the prophecies that came to pass in a literal fashion when Jesus came the first time would set the pattern for how the prophecies connected to His second coming would come to pass? There is no place for splitting up these interpretations. So, in answer to the question: Is the Old Testament Amillennial? Of course not. If you affirm a normal hermeneutic and the perspicuity of the Old Testament, it pronounces clearly covenants and promises and a kingdom to come to ethnic Israel.

I am not going to have time to develop all of this, but I want you to just think for a minute about the Old Testament covenants so that you understand something of their nature. The Old Testament must be interpreted, preached and taught as clear revelation from God that is to be understood, believed and applied by the people to whom it was given. So what did God promise Israel? Let's look at the twelfth chapter of Genesis. Obviously this is a study beyond our capability to dig into all the details [in this lecture]; but it's clear, it's not difficult, it is straightforward. I want you to see the connection between these covenants and divine, electing sovereignty.

In Genesis 12 we read, "The Lord said to Abram, 'Go forth from your country and from your relatives and from your father's house.'" Now there you have a great illustration of election; that's almost like a Damascus road experience, isn't it? What did Abraham, or Abram as he is called here, do to set this in motion? Nothing. Abram plays no part in this covenant. Now follow the use of the expression, "I will." "And *I will* make you a great nation. And *I will* bless you and make your name great and so you shall be a blessing. And *I will* bless those who bless you and the one who curses you *I will* curse, and in you all the families of the earth shall be blessed." "I will." "I will." "I will." "I will." "I will." Five times [including the end of verse 1]. Sovereign, unilateral, unconditional election.

To seal that, go to the fifteenth chapter of Genesis, and this, by the way, is repeated in the thirteenth and seventeenth chapters and on through to the patriarchs who followed Abram. But in the fifteenth chapter it's wonderful to see the picture here, starting in verse 8. Abram wants a little bit of confirmation; this is a big step, "So Lord God how may I know that I shall possess it?" How do I know this is really going to happen? So this is what God said, "'Bring me a three year old heifer, a three year old female goat, a three year old ram, a turtledove and a young pigeon.' He brought all these to Him, cut them in two, laid each half opposite the other. He didn't cut the birds"—it would just be a pile of feathers [laughter from audience] —and "the birds of prey came down upon the carcasses and Abram drove them away." So now what has he done? He has taken these animals; he has cut them in half; he set them opposite each other; he has a little path going through these split animals and the two dead birds, one on each side. This relates to the term in Hebrew to "cut a covenant." When you "cut a covenant" you put blood sacrifices as a way to demonstrate the seriousness and to bind yourself, as it were, by blood to fulfill your promise. So God prepares what would be a very traditional, very typical way to engage in making a covenant. Only this is very different because in verse 12 as the sun was going down; a deep sleep fell upon Abram; God anesthetized him. Terror and great darkness fell upon him, and God said to Abram, "Know for certain that your descendants will be strangers in a land that is not theirs where they will be enslaved and oppressed four hundred years." Four hundred meant four hundred!

Well, God puts him to sleep and God says this is what is going to happen. Verse 14, "I will also judge the nations whom they will serve, and afterward they will come out with many possessions. As for you, you shall go to your fathers in peace; you will be buried at a good old age," and so forth. And then down in to verse 17, "It came about when the sun had set, and it was very dark, and behold, there appeared a smoking oven and a flaming torch which passed between these pieces." God put Abram out, anesthetized him, and God alone went through the pieces—unilateral, unconditional, irrevocable promise that God made with Himself. There were no conditions for Abraham on his own to fulfill. On that day the Lord made a covenant with Abram. It is to be a covenant that does not end. Chapter 17 verse 7, "I will establish my covenant between me and you and your descendants after you throughout your generations for an everlasting covenant to be God to you and to your descendants after you." God elected Abram, elected the nation that would come out of His loins, and made a covenant and a promise with them to be their God. This is the foundational covenant in the Bible—the foundational biblical covenant, the promise of God, unilateral and unconditional. When God later gave the Mosaic covenant, it became very apparent how sinful Israel was. Even in the midst of Israel's blatant sin, apostasy, idolatry, violation of God's law, they still continued to be the object of His covenant love [on the basis of the Abrahamic covenant].

Read Ezekiel 16. In Ezekiel 16 there is this staggering chronicle by God of His choice of Israel. And I can't take you all through it, but He talks in graphic terms about electing Israel like finding a baby thrown away in a field. Verse 4, "...on the day you were born your naval cord was not cut nor were you washed with water for cleansing; You were not rubbed with salt" —which they did as a disinfectant—"or even wrapped in cloths. No one looked with pity on you to do any of these things. No one had compassion on you. You were thrown out in an open field, abhorred the day you were born. [God says,] 'I passed by you, I saw you squirming in your blood. I said to you while you were in your blood, Live! I said to you while you were in your blood, Live!'" There again is that sovereign election. And then the story goes on about how God took Israel and, as it were, married Israel, cleaned Israel up, made Israel His people. If you go over to verse 28, "...you played the harlot with the Assyrians because you were not satisfied, you even played the harlot with them and still you were not satisfied." You had an insatiable lust for adultery with other gods and other people. "...your lewdness," verse 36, "poured out, your nakedness was uncovered, your harlotries with your lovers, all of your detestable idols," just indictment after indictment after indictment. God is furious with them. But you come down to the end of the chapter, "Nevertheless," verse 60, "I will remember My covenant with you in the days of your youth."

What attribute of God does that describe? His faithfulness. "I will establish an everlasting covenant with you, you will remember your ways and be ashamed when you receive your sisters, your older, your younger, I will give them to you as daughters but not because of your covenant. Thus I will establish My covenant with you. You shall know that I am the Lord in order that you may remember and be ashamed and never open your mouth anymore because of your humiliation, when I have forgiven you for all that you have done," the Lord God says. Wow, a reiteration of the terms of the covenant in the face of Israel's history of defection, disobedience and apostasy. Israel is like Gomer, right? The prostitute. The harlot. Listen, God's decision to set His love on Israel was in no way determined by Israel's performance; not determined by Israel's national worthiness—purely on the basis of His independent, uninfluenced, sovereign grace. Read Deuteronomy 7:7 and 8. He chose them because He predetermined to set His love on them for no other reason—election. The survival of the kingdom of Judah, despite the blatant sin of its rulers, depended on covenant promises God had made. Read Psalm 89. Read Psalm 132 where these are reiterated. God's unilateral covenant declares that the Lord alone is the sole party responsible to fulfill the obligations. There are no conditions which Abram or any other Jew could fulfill on his own. It's no different than your salvation—you were chosen. But you didn't come to Christ on your own. You were given life by the Spirit of God in God's time. God's unilateral covenant declares that the Lord alone is the sole party responsible to fulfill the obligations.

Now listen to it this way, obedience is not the condition that determines fulfillment. Divine sovereign power is the condition that determines obedience which leads to fulfillment. When God gave the unilateral covenant, He knew He would have to produce the obedience in the future, according to His plan. And He gave the Davidic covenant in 2 Samuel 7 in which promise comes to David that he will have a greater son who will have an everlasting kingdom. That is an expansion, by the way, of the Abrahamic covenant. Verses 12–13, just quickly, read, "...I will establish his kingdom. He shall build a house for My name, I will establish the throne of his kingdom forever." God promises to Abram a seed, a land, a nation—and of course that embodies a kingdom—and now comes the promise of a king. This is an expansion of the Abrahamic covenant; and what's notable here, again, in verses 12–13 of 2 Samuel 7: "*I will* raise up your descendant... *I will* establish his kingdom... *I will* establish the throne of his kingdom forever." "I will," "I will," "I will," again. This is not to say that the Abrahamic covenant is only for Israel. We all participate in its blessings, spiritually, and we will millennially. We all will participate in the Abrahamic and the Davidic covenants because we'll participate in salvation and be in the kingdom.

There's a third covenant, the New Covenant, and this one I do want to draw to your attention. Jeremiah 31 indicates that there can be no fulfillment of the promises God gave to Abraham or David apart from salvation. Through history there has always been an Israel of God, there has always been a remnant, there have always been those who did not bow the knee to Baal. God always has had a people; there have always been His chosen ones. Not all Israel is Israel; that is to say, not all of ethnic Israel is the true Israel of God, true believers. But God has always had a remnant; He has always had a people--as Isaiah 6 says, a "stump," a "holy seed"--throughout history. But in the future there will be a salvation of ethnic Israel on a national level, and that's the message of Jeremiah 31.

Here is the New Covenant; it was also given to Israel. We like to talk about the New Covenant because we participate in the salvation provision of the New Covenant ratified in the death of Christ. But the original pledge of the New Covenant is in a special way given to a future generation of Jews. Listen to verse 31, "'Behold days are coming,' declares the Lord, 'when I will make a new covenant with the house of Israel and with the house of Judah.'" That is unmistakable. "'...not like the covenant I made with their fathers the day I took them by the hand to bring them out of the land of Egypt....'" Not like that Mosaic covenant; that was not a saving covenant. "'My covenant, which they broke although I was a husband to them,' declares the Lord, 'But this is the covenant which I will make again with the house of Israel.'" What warrant is there to say that does not mean Israel? It *does* mean Israel. "I will." "I will." "I will." "I will." "*I will* make the covenant with the house of Israel." "*I will* put My law within them and on their heart. *I will* write it; and *I will* be their God, and they shall be My people." End of verse 34, "... *I will* forgive their iniquity, and their sin *I will* remember no more." Did you ever see so many *I will*'s? They are all over the place. This covenant is unconditional, unilateral, sovereign, gracious, and irrevocable.

You say, "Well maybe God changed His mind." Go to verse 35, "Thus says the Lord, 'Who gives the sun for light by day and a fixed order of the moon and the stars for light by night, Who stirs up the sea so that its waves roar; the Lord of hosts is His name: If this fixed order departs from before Me,' declares the Lord, 'Then the offspring of Israel also shall cease.'" I haven't noticed that that's happened, have you? Has anybody noticed that? There isn't any other way to understand that. If it doesn't mean what it just said, it is incomprehensible. And the New Covenant promises the salvation that then includes the reception of all the promises in the Abrahamic and Davidic covenants and all the extended promises throughout the whole Old Testament.

And what is the key feature of this? "I will put My Law within them. On their heart I will write it. I will be their God. I will forgive their iniquity." You see how sovereign that is? "*I will* do it, *I will* do it in my time." Look at Ezekiel 36 because this is a parallel. I know it's familiar to you, but I think it's good to just be reminded. Ezekiel 36:24, "For *I will* take you from the nations, gather you from all the lands, bring you into your own land. Then *I will* sprinkle clean water on you and you will be clean; *I will* cleanse you from all your filthiness and from all your idols. Moreover, *I will* give you a new heart and put a new spirit within you. and *I will* remove the heart of stone from your flesh and give you a heart of flesh. *I will* put My spirit within you...." It's overwhelming, isn't it? "...cause you to walk in My statutes, you will be careful to observe My ordinances." How could anybody walk in His statutes and obey and observe His ordinances? Only if He caused you to do it. And "You will live in the land that I gave your forefathers; so you will be My people and I will be your God."

And then verse 32—just a good reminder, "I am not doing this for your sake." Huh? He's not doing this for your sake? "...let it be known to you. Be ashamed and confounded for your ways, O house of Israel!" So for whose sake is He doing it? His own. Go to the end of verse 38, "When I do this, then they will know that I am the Lord." You can read the 37th verse. Same thing.

So when God gave unilateral, unconditional, sovereign, gracious promises to an elect people guaranteed by divine faithfulness to be fulfilled like all His salvation work by divine power, and when God says such covenant promises are irrevocable, we cannot without impunity and guilt for any seemingly convenient idea or assumption say that those promises are void.

Why? You say, "Well what about Israel's apostasy? Doesn't that cancel the promises? Doesn't Israel's apostasy cancel the promises?" Do you understand that the New Covenant promises given in Jeremiah and Ezekiel were given to Israel at the time when they were under divine judgment for apostasy? They weren't given to them when all was well and they were living and flourishing in obedience to God. They were so apostate they were out of their land, and then the covenant was given to them and God was saying, "Don't get the idea that what's going on by way of apostasy changes My promises."

You say, "Wait a minute, didn't they reject their Lord and Messiah? That did it. They rejected him; they killed Jesus." But that's in the plan. One of the wacky ideas of Dispensationalism is that Jesus came and offered a kingdom, and because the Jews didn't accept it and killed Him, He went to the Church. He came up with Plan B. The Cross is not Plan B. What do you think Zechariah 12:10 is saying when it says, "...they will look on Him whom they have pierced?" Read Psalm 22. It describes the Crucifixion. Read Isaiah 53. It describes the Crucifixion. It's in the plan. In Zechariah 12:10, Zechariah says, "they will look on him whom they have pierced," and then in chapter 13 verse 1, a fountain of cleansing will be opened to Israel. Israel will be saved, the New Covenant will be fulfilled, and you keep reading into chapter 14, and the kingdom comes. There is no other way to interpret Zechariah 12–14.

So, is the Old Testament Amill? No.

II. Were the Jews in Jesus' day Amillennialists? No. Consider Emil Schurer's helpful study of Jewish eschatology in the day of Jesus published in 1880 by T & T Clark in Edinburgh—a new edition of it came out in 1998 by Hendrickson Publishing. He does a great job of studying the Jewish Messianic eschatological mindset at the time of Jesus. . . . They believed that the Messiah was coming, preceded by a time of trouble. They believed that before Messiah, Elijah the prophet would come. They believed that when Messiah came, He would be the personal Son of David, He would have special powers to set up His kingdom, and all Abrahamic covenant and Davidic covenant promises would be fulfilled. They also believed that Israel would repent and be saved at the coming of

Messiah. They believed the kingdom would be established in Israel with Jerusalem at the center and would extend across the world. They believed that peace and righteousness would dominate the world, all people would worship the Messiah, there would be no war—only gladness and health. They believed in a re-instituted temple worship, and the fulfillment of the covenants included the renovation of the world, a general resurrection, final judgment and after that the eternal state. That's Jewish pre-New Testament eschatology. Dead on target. That's what Zacharias the priestly father of John the Baptist believed. Read Zacharias' great benedictus in Luke 1:67 to the end of the chapter, and what is he saying? Every single phrase in that comes from an Old Testament text on the Abrahamic covenant, the Davidic covenant, or the New Covenant. Every single one of them. He knew what was happening. The covenants were to be fulfilled.

III. Was Jesus an Amillennialist? Turn to Acts 1. This has just been sitting there for a long time, and I don't know if we always look closely at these things. This is post-Resurrection, "The first account," verse 1, "I composed, Theophilus about all that Jesus began to do and teach until the day when He was taken up after He had by the Holy Spirit given orders to the apostles whom He had chosen." There is that election again. So, he had spent time before His ascension with the apostles. Now verse 3, "To these He also presented Himself alive after His suffering by many convincing proofs appearing to them over a period of forty days." Literally appearing to them over forty days. It must have been intense. Can you imagine the level of teaching a resurrected Jesus would give His own over a forty-day period? What kind of a seminary education would that be? And what was He talking about? "...speaking of the things concerning the kingdom of God." Oh, this is perfect! For forty days He talked about the kingdom of God. This is His moment. If Jesus is an Amillennialist, this is where He has to tell them. Their [Israel's] apostasy—that's a given. Their rejection of the Messiah— that's a given. The execution of the Messiah—that's a given. This is the perfect place for Jesus to launch Amillennialism.

Go down to verse 6. "So when they had come together, they were asking Him saying, 'Lord, is it at this time you are restoring the kingdom to Israel?'" Now, what do you think He said? "Where did you get such a stupid idea? Where did you ever come up with that concept? Haven't you been listening for forty days? I'm an Amillennialist. What a bizarre thought—that I am going to restore the kingdom to Israel! You don't listen." This is it. If Jesus is Amillennial, this is His moment! He's got to say, "No, the Church is the new Israel." The disciples were asking if this is the time the Father is going to restore [the kingdom], according to Jewish sources the technical eschatological term for the end time—they were using a term that was a part of their eschatology. Is this the end time when You are restoring the kingdom to Israel? Forty days of instruction on the kingdom, and they knew one thing for sure, the kingdom for Israel was still coming. And all they wanted to know was, what's the question? WHEN? That's all. And He said to them, "It's not for you to know the times or seasons." You can't know timing. He didn't say "Wait, wait, wait, there isn't going to be a kingdom." He said, "It's not for you to know times and seasons which the Father has"—what?—"fixed by His own authority." There's that sovereign election again. It's sovereign. They knew that. "Lord, is it at this time you are restoring the kingdom?" They knew that it was a divine work to do it.

This is a perfect opportunity for Jesus to straighten things out. Dig a little into the text, verse 7, "which the Father has fixed." *Tithemi*: set, appointed. I love this. "Fixed" is in the aorist middle— "fixed for Himself." Fixed for Himself. It's about His glory. Right? It's about His exaltation. It's about the whole world finally seeing paradise regained. It's about God finally being glorified, who is so dishonored throughout human history. It's about the glory of God and the honor of Jesus Christ. And God the Father has fixed for Himself that time by His own authority. It is singular, unilateral. There is no other way to understand it. There's no replacement theology in the theology of Jesus! There's no supersessionism.

This [supersessionism] is a movement to establish that there is no earthly kingdom for Israel. That is absolutely foreign to the Old Testament and completely foreign to the New Testament. Jesus didn't say, "Where'd you get that crazy idea? Haven't you been listening?" They just couldn't know the season, the time. The Cross was always the plan. He said in the eighteenth chapter of Luke, also recorded in Matthew and Mark, "We're going to Jerusalem. And you know what's going to happen?" If you put those three accounts together, "I'm going to be betrayed, I'm going to be handed over to the chief priests and the scribes, they're going to condemn me, they're going to hand me over to the Gentiles because they can't execute me." All this is in exact order. "Then when I'm handed over to the Gentiles, I'm going to be mocked, mistreated, spit on, scourged, crucified, and I'm rising again." That's not Plan B. In fact, if you think that's Plan B, you're a fool! And Jesus called you one, "Oh foolish men and slow of heart to believe in all that the prophets have spoken," Luke 24:25.

So wherever Amillennialism came from, it didn't come from the Old Testament, it didn't come from New Testament Jews, and it didn't come from Jesus.

IV. You say, "Well, were the apostles Amillennial? How about Peter—was Peter Amillennial?" Maybe Peter was the first Amillennialist. Look at Acts 3:12. I love this. Peter is preaching away, "Men of Israel," and so forth. Verse 13, "The God of Abraham, Isaac, and Jacob, the God of our fathers, has glorified His servant Jesus, the one whom you delivered up" —there's that primary and secondary element— "...and disowned in the presence of Pilate, whom he decided to release to you, you disowned the Holy and Righteous One and asked for a murderer to be granted to you, but put to death the Prince of life." Oh my, what an indictment! It couldn't be any worse; it couldn't be any more horrific! Look what you've done! Verse 18, "But the things which God announced beforehand by the mouth of all the prophets, that His Christ should suffer, He has thus fulfilled." That's literal, isn't it?! "Repent therefore and return, that your sins may be wiped away in order that times of refreshing may come from the presence of the Lord." The "times of refreshing" is a kingdom phrase. "...[T]hat He may send Jesus, the Christ appointed for you" —set for you, fixed for you— "whom heaven must receive until the period of restoration"— another kingdom term—"of all things about which God spoke by the mouth of His holy prophets from ancient time." And then I especially love verse 25, "And it is you who are the sons of the prophets and of the covenant which God made with your fathers." Does Peter cancel the covenant? What does he say? "You are the sons of the covenant which God made with your fathers, saying to Abraham, 'In your seed shall all the families of the earth be blessed,' For you first, God raised up His servant, Christ, sent Him to bless you by turning every one of you from your wicked ways."

And He will do that; you're still the sons of the covenant. This would have been a perfect opportunity for Peter to cancel those promises if indeed they had been canceled.

What about James, the head of the Jerusalem church? Was he Amillennial in his view? In the fifteenth chapter of Acts and verse 13, James answered, "Brethren, listen to me. Simeon has related how God first concerned Himself about taking from among the Gentiles a people for His name. And with this the words of the Prophets agree, just as it is written: 'After these things I will return, I will rebuild the tabernacle of David which has fallen, and I will rebuild its ruins, and I will restore it, in order that the rest of mankind may seek the Lord, and all the Gentiles who are called by My name,' says the Lord, 'Who make these things known from of old.'" The acceptance of the Gentiles is not the cancellation of promises to Israel. After Gentile conversion, after the times of the Gentiles are over, "I will rebuild the tabernacle of David which has fallen, ...rebuild its ruins, and...restore it." The Davidic covenant promises, and the Messianic promises will be fulfilled.

Maybe the writer of Hebrews was an Amillennialist. Chapter 6, verse 13: "...when God made the promise to Abraham, since He could swear by no greater, He swore by Himself, saying 'I will surely bless you, I will surely multiply you.'" "I will. I will." No hesitation. And He calls on our understanding of swearing. "...men swear by one greater than themselves, with them an oath given as confirmation is an end of every dispute. In the same way God, desiring more to show to the heirs of the promise the unchangeableness of His purpose, interposed with an oath." God swears; He makes an oath! And it is "...impossible," the next verse says, "for God to lie."

Maybe the apostle Paul was the first Amillennialist. Look at Romans 3:1—"...what advantage has the Jew? Or what benefit of circumcision? Great in every respect. First of all...they were entrusted with the oracles of God. What then? If some did not believe, their unbelief will not nullify the faithfulness of God, will it? May it never be!" And this is where Paul should have said, "Absolutely! Absolutely it nullifies the promise of God! Unquestionably it nullifies the promise of God!" But he doesn't say that. Chapter 9, and verse 6: "...it is not as though the word of God has failed. For they are not all Israel who are descended from

Israel." That is to say, they are not all true Israel, that is, true believers. "...[N]or are they all children because they are Abraham's descendants, but: 'Through Isaac your descendants will be named.' That is, it is not the children of the flesh who are children of God, but the children of promise are regarded as descendants." And He goes on to describe it, saying something as blatant as this, "Jacob I loved"— verse 13—"Esau I hated." Verse 1, "I'll have mercy on whom I'll have mercy, I'll have compassion on whom I have compassion." Verse 16, "....it doesn't depend on the man who wills or the man who runs, but on God who has mercy." Verse 18, "He has mercy on whom He desires, He hardens whom He desires." This is back to this whole idea of sovereignty again! The fact that there are some Jews who don't believe does not nullify the faithfulness of God. Just because there are some whom God chooses, doesn't mean that He's not going to choose a whole, duly-constituted generation of Jews to fulfill His promises [in the future].

And then, perhaps most notably (and we're hurrying a little bit), Romans 11:26, "...all Israel will be saved." How can you interpret that? There is only one way! You tell me that's not Israel?! Where in the text does it say it's not Israel? I would understand if it said, "And God has cancelled His promises to Israel." But it says all Israel will be saved just as it is written "The Deliverer will come from Zion, will remove ungodliness from Jacob. This is My covenant with them when I take away their sins." Yes, they are enemies at the present time, but that is for the sake of the Gentiles. Verse 29, "...the gifts and the calling of God are irrevocable." And now we're back to where we started, right? Look, the promise might be cancelled if it depended on them to obey on their own, but that was impossible from the start. Only the One who made the promise can enable the obedience that is connected to the fulfillment of the promise.

Now much more could be said about Romans 11. So when Jonathan Edwards wrote this: "Promises that were made by the prophets to the people of Israel concerning their future prosperity and glory are fulfilled in the Christian Church according to their proper intent." I say, where did he get that? Where did that come from? It did not come from any passage that I can find.

Let me just conclude with some effects and there is a lot more I could say. That's what we always say when we've just run out of material. [Laughter from audience] You've really endured lengthy presentation—but just a couple more comments.

I suggest for your reading *Israel and the Church* by Ronald Diprose. We should have some in the bookstore. It first appeared in Italian. It was a Ph.D. dissertation. It has no connection to traditional Dispensationalism. It's a really fine work on replacement theology. It shows the effect of this idea as forming the Church of the Dark Ages, explaining how the Church went from the New Testament concept of the Church to the sacerdotal, sacramental institutional system of the Dark Ages that we know as Roman Catholicism. Diprose lays much of that at the feet of the replacement theology that rises out of Augustine and the few before him; Origen and Justin.

Where did the Church ever come up with altars? There is no altar in the New Testament. Where did the Church ever come up with sacrifices? Where did the Church ever come up with a parallel sign to circumcision? Where did the Church ever come up with the priesthood? Where did the Church ever come up with ceremony and ritual and symbolism? Where did the Church ever come up with the idea that you should reintroduce mystery by speaking in a language that the people there couldn't understand? They replaced preaching with ritual. From the formation of the Church in those early centuries to the system of Roman Catholicism, all the trappings fit Old Testament Judaism. And the hierarchical, institutional, non-personal, non-organic, sacerdotal approach to the Church he [Diprose] traces largely to the influence of causing the Church to be the new Israel. Replacement theology justifies bringing in all the trappings of Judaism.

Another effect of replacement theology is the damage that it does to Jewish evangelism. Here is a little scenario: You are talking to a Jew.

You say, "Jesus is the Messiah."
He says, "Really, where is the kingdom?"
"Oh, it's here!"
"Oh, it is? Well, why are we being killed all the time? Why are we being persecuted and why don't we have the land that was promised to us? And why isn't the Messiah reigning in Jerusalem, and why isn't peace and joy and gladness

dominating the world, and why isn't the desert blooming and...?"

"Oh, no, you don't understand. All that's not going to happen. You see, the problem is you're not God's people any more. We are."

"Oh! I see, but this is the kingdom, and Jews are being killed and hated, and Jerusalem is under siege. This is the kingdom? If this is the kingdom, Jesus is not the Messiah. He can't be. It's ludicrous."

No matter how many wonderful Jewish-Christian relationships we try to have with rabbis, this is a huge bone in the throat. Why can't Jesus be the Messiah? Because this isn't the kingdom. Unless you can say to a Jew, "God will keep every single promise He made to you, and Jesus will fulfill every single promise, and that is why there are still Jews in the world, and that is why you are in the land and God is preparing for a great day of salvation in Israel; and Jesus is your Messiah. But look at Psalm 22 and Isaiah 53 and Zechariah 12:10 and understand that He had to come and die to ratify the New Covenant before He could forgive your sin, and the kingdom is coming," you don't have a chance to communicate! The rest doesn't make sense.

Now, if you get election right—divine, sovereign, gracious, unconditional, unilateral, irrevocable election—and you get God right, and you get Israel right, and you get eschatology right, then guess what, men, you can just open your Bible and preach your heart out of that text and say what it says. How freeing is that? You don't have to scramble around and find some bizarre interpretation. Get it right and God is glorified. Get it right and Christ is exalted. Get it right and the Holy Spirit is honored. Get it right and Scripture is clear. Get it right and the greatest historical illustration of God's work in the world is visible. Get it right and the meaning of mystery in the New Testament is maintained. Get it right and normal language is intact and Scripture wasn't written for mystics. Get it right and the chronology of prophetic literature is intact. Get it right and you shut out imagination from exegesis. Get it right and a historical worldview is complete. Get it right and the practical benefit of eschatology is released on your people. Get it right.

The kingdom theology of the eschaton is the only view that honors sovereign electing grace, honors the truthfulness of God's promises, honors the teaching of Old Testament prophets, the teaching of Jesus and the New Testament writers; and that will allow Christ to be honored as supreme ruler over His creation now temporarily in the hands of Satan. And the earthly millennial kingdom established at Christ's return is the only and necessary bridge from temporary human history to eternal divine glory. Make your church a second coming church and make your life a second coming life.

Let's pray. Father, what a day for us to begin! What a glorious transcendent theme! May we live in the light of the coming of Christ. May we know that the Word can be trusted, and that we can preach every verse and say, "This is what it says. This is what it means." And thus give glory to You. Thank You for these precious men who are here. Lord fill us all with joy in the truth and in the privilege of serving You. In Christ's name. Amen.

Scripture Index

Name and Subject Index

Printed in the USA
CPSIA information can be obtained
at www.ICGtesting.com
LVHW081351110124
768640LV00014B/992